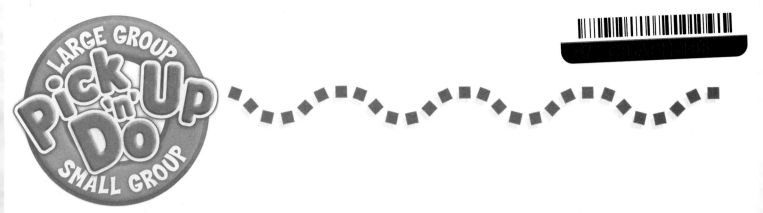

Rise and Shine!
The Early Church

12 Instant Bible Lessons
for Kids

Edited by Mary Grace Becker

NEXGEN®

Building the New Generation of Believers

An Imprint of Cook Communications Ministries
COLORADO SPRINGS, COLORADO • PARIS, ONTARIO
KINGSWAY COMMUNICATIONS, LTD., EASTBOURNE, ENGLAND

Pick Up 'n' Do: Rise and Shine! The Early Church
Copyright © 2006 Cook Communications Ministries

Editor: Mary Grace Becker
Writers: Scharlotte Rich, Faye Spieker
Art Direction: Nancy L. Haskins
Cover Design: Helen Harrison
Photos © Gaylon Wampler Photography
Interior Design: Helen Harrison, Nancy L. Haskins, Lois Keffer
Illustrators: Kris and Sharon Cartwright and Marilee Harrald-Pilz

Printed in Canada

First printing, 2006
1 2 3 4 5 6 7 8 9 10   09 08 07 06

ISBN 10: 0–7814–4376–8
ISBN 13: 978–07814–4376–0

Table of Contents

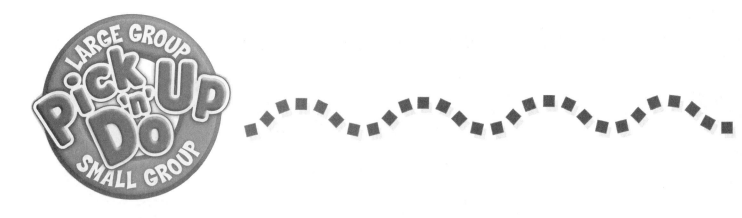

Quick Start Guide

Pick Up 'n' Do elementary lessons give your kids great Bible teaching and serious discipleship without hours of preparation. You and your kids will love these large group/small group lessons. Two options let you take the lesson from super simple to more challenging.

If you're looking for an "instant" lesson that you can pick up and do at the last minute, you've got it in Bible 4U! and Shepherd's Spot.

All you need is a photocopier and basic classroom supplies such as pencils, scissors and glue sticks. Copy the **Bible 4U!** instant drama and the **Shepherd's Spot** handout, and you're ready to go.

Are you looking for something beyond the basics?

The optional **Get Set** section of the lessons gives you an opportunity to get a puppet into the action. "Schooner" is a mouthy macaw whose bright remarks will bring giggles and grins each week. And he does a smack-up job of setting up the Bible story.

Don't have a puppet ministry team in your church? How about recruiting middle schoolers? The lively back and forth between Schooner and the Leader is right up their alley. What a great way to get them involved in ministry to younger children!

Now for the heart of the lesson

Bible 4U!

The Bible is full of drama! What better way to teach than with fascinating dramas that take a unique approach to each Bible story? Photocopy the instant drama, pull volunteers from your group to read the roles, and you're ready to go.

You'll keep your knowledgeable students engaged, and give kids who are new to God's Word a solid foundation of biblical truth. The dramas call for just a few characters. You may want to play the main role yourself. Or call on a teen or adult drama troupe to prepare and present the dramas each week. Either way, kids will see the Bible stories come to life in unforgettable ways.

Shepherd's Spot

This is the second essential step of the lesson. After **Bible 4U!**, kids break into small groups with one adult helper for every 8 to 10 kids. Nothing leaves a more indelible impact on kids' lives than the warm, personal touch of a caring adult. The instructions and handouts, which may be copied, (we suggest bright copy paper) will give your helpers the confidence they need to help kids consider how to live out what they've learned.

In the **Shepherd's Spot**, kids will read the story straight from the Bible. They'll learn basic Bible skills, and complete a fun handout that helps them understand how to get the story off the page and into their lives. They'll close each week by sharing concerns and praying together.

Workshop Wonders

And there's more! Each week, the optional **Workshop Wonders** section gives you a game, craft, science, or cooking activity that gets your kids out of their chairs and into the action.

The **Workshop Wonders** activities require more than the usual classroom supplies. If you choose one of these activities, you'll need to pick up cooking or science ingredients or a few simple craft or game supplies. If you don't mind a little extra preparation, you'll find that there's nothing like a little hands-on action to bring that moment of learning wonder to kids' faces.

These special activities are guaranteed to make a memory and help the Bible lesson stick with kids for a long time to come.

That's it! You can go for a quick, simple lesson with **Bible 4U!** and the **Shepherd's Spot**.

If you wish, add another level of excitement and learning with the Schooner script in the optional **Get Set** section of each lesson.

And if you love teaching with activities, do a little shopping and give kids the memorable experiences of **Workshop Wonders**.

1. Bible 4U!

2. Shepherd's Spot

Do you want to give your kids even more great stuff?

How About Staff?

Finding Schooner

If you do the **Get Set** option to open the lessons, you'll need to purchase a parrot or scarlet macaw puppet.

You'll find a great selection on the Internet, in all sizes and prices. Type "scarlet macaw puppet" into your favorite search engine and browse until you find the puppet that suits your price range.

You need just a few helpers to make Pick Up 'n' Do lessons a great experience for you and your kids!

1. A leader/emcee hosts the **Bible 4U!** instant drama each week. For a quick presentation, pull kids from your group to read the roles in the dramas. When there are just one or two parts, you may want to step into the leading role yourself.

2. You may wish to ask a small drama troupe to prepare the stories each week. Five or six volunteers who serve on a rotating basis can easily cover the stories with just a few minutes' preparation.

3. For the **Shepherd's Spot**, you'll need one adult leader for every eight to ten kids. You'll need caring adults in this role—people who are good listeners and feel comfortable sharing their lives with kids. This is a great first step into children's ministry for adults who haven't taught before.

4. If you choose to do the optional **Get Set** puppet script, you'll need a leader and a puppeteer. It's best to use the same leader who hosts the Bible dramas. If you recruit a couple of people to play Schooner, they can rotate every few weeks.

For Overachievers

Do you have a great stage set-up at your church? Then you may want to go for some flash and glitz. Give Schooner a little tropical cabana with a palm tree and a sea-breezy backdrop. Make sure your leader has an obnoxious tropical shirt to slip on.

Don't forget the music! Warm kids up each week with lively, interactive praise songs. Then bring on Schooner's set to the tune of island rhythms.

Equip your drama troupe with a box full of Bibletime costumes. You'll find tips for props and staging in the "for Overachievers" box just before each Bible story. Of course, all this pizzazz is purely optional. The most important ingredient in a wonderful Bible lesson is YOU—the warm, caring leader whose love for kids calls you into children's ministry in the first place! There is absolutely no substitute for the personal attention you give to children each week. You become the model of Jesus himself through your gifts of time and commitment.

God bless you as you minister to his kids!

Up, Up, and Away!

Option

Get Set
LARGE GROUP ■ Greet kids and do a puppet skit. Schooner discovers that good news is made for sharing.
❏ large bird puppet ❏ puppeteer

1

Bible 4U! Instant Drama
LARGE GROUP ■ Eager to get the scoop, reporters interview eyewitnesses over the buzz that Jesus ascended to heaven.
❏ 4 actors ❏ copies of pp. 10–11, "Good News!" script ❏ 4 numbered balls
Optional: ❏ hats ❏ pencils ❏ notebooks ❏ tape recorder ❏ camera
❏ Bibletime clothes and sandals ❏ backdrop of a Bibletime town

2

Shepherd's Spot
SMALL GROUP ■ Finish writing a newspaper, the "Jerusalem Daily Trumpet," to encourage kids to speak to others about the love of Jesus. Share concerns and pray together. Send home the Special Delivery handout.
❏ Bibles ❏ pencils ❏ scissors ❏ copies of p. 14, "Jerusalem Daily Trumpet"
❏ copies of p. 16, Special Delivery ❏ ribbon or twine

Option

Workshop Wonders *
SMALL GROUP ■ Make a snack cup where fruit ascends as a reminder of today's Bible story.
❏ foam cups ❏ straws ❏ spray whipped cream ❏ ripe strawberries pieces or grapes ❏ plastic spoons and knives ❏ paper towels

*Check with parents for any food allergies children may have.

Bible Basis
Jesus ascends to heaven.
Acts 1:1–11

Learn It!
God gives us the power to do his work.

Live It!
Witness to others.

Bible Verse
"You will be my witnesses in Jerusalem, and in all Judea and Samaria, and to the ends of the earth." Acts 1:8

Quick Takes

Acts 1:1–11

1:1 In my former book, Theophilus, I wrote about all that Jesus began to do and to teach 2 until the day he was taken up to heaven, after giving instructions through the Holy Spirit to the apostles he had chosen. 3 After his suffering, he showed himself to these men and gave many convincing proofs that he was alive. He appeared to them over a period of forty days and spoke about the kingdom of God. 4 On one occasion, while he was eating with them, he gave them this command: "Do not leave Jerusalem, but wait for the gift my Father promised, which you have heard me speak about. 5 For John baptized with water, but in a few days you will be baptized with the Holy Spirit." 6 So when they met together, they asked him, "Lord, are you at this time going to restore the kingdom to Israel?"

7 He said to them: "It is not for you to know the times or dates the Father has set by his own authority. 8 "But you will receive power when the Holy Spirit comes on you; and you will be my witnesses in Jerusalem, and in all Judea and Samaria, and to the ends of the earth." 9 After he said this, he was taken up before their very eyes, and a cloud hid him from their sight. 10 They were looking intently up into the sky as he was going, when suddenly two men dressed in white stood beside them. 11 "Men of Galilee," they said, "why do you stand here looking into the sky? This same Jesus, who has been taken from you into heaven, will come back in the same way you have seen him go into heaven."

Insights

Luke, a doctor who traveled with Paul, wrote the book of Acts. He was an intelligent man, meticulous at keeping an account of the facts of all the wonderful yet unusual things that were happening during this time. The Book of Acts starts in Jerusalem, with Jesus ascending into heaven, and ends with Paul locked up in Rome, the biggest city of the time. Sandwiched in between are stories incredible beyond imagination.

The book picks up the story of Jesus 40 days after he rose from the dead. Jesus appeared to hundreds of people during this period of time, proving that he was alive and continuing to preach the kingdom of God. He now tells his close followers not to leave Jerusalem, but to wait to be baptized with the power of the Holy Spirit. They will be witnesses to the entire world, beginning in Jerusalem where they had gathered, and spreading from there all the way to the ends of the earth.

The scope of the Book of Acts covers 30 years—critical years for the early church, years during which the disciples did, in fact, carry the good news of Jesus far and wide. The rest of Acts relates great examples of God's power. After being baptized by the Holy Spirit, the believers become stronger in their faith. Thousands of people believe in Jesus. People are healed, Peter and John are freed from prison by an angel, Paul becomes a believer and missionary after persecuting Christians. What an exciting time!

Option Get Set

Hello, everyone! Gather and sit down. Today's story is simply incredible—Jesus rising through the clouds and into heaven. If you saw it yourself, you would never forget it. It would inspire you to tell others about what you saw—once you got over your amazement. I wonder how Schooner feels about sharing incredible news. Schooner! *Schooner pops up.*

Schooner: *(excited)* Squawk! Squawk!

Leader: What is it, Schooner? Calm down!

Schooner: Boss, I just saw the best video! It was so cool. You should see it.

Leader: Really? Tell me about it.

Schooner: Dinosaurs, with 3-D special effects. Things jump out at you and you have to duck because you're sure they'll hit you! *(ducks)*

Leader: That does sound cool.

Schooner: Yeah, and the video has high-flying pterodactyls in it. They did some fantastic tricks, zooming over canyons and mountains. *(ruffles feathers)*

Leader: It sounds exciting.

Schooner: My friend Sam first told me about it.

Leader: Sam? Isn't that the friend you hoped someday would visit us?

Schooner: Yep, that's the guy.

Leader: Did you ask him to visit today?

Schooner: Oh, no! I didn't want to impose on him.

Leader: Wait a minute, what do you mean, "impose on him"?

Schooner: You know, church, religion and stuff. Religion is personal, boss. I wouldn't want to tell him what to do, or where he should go. *(excitedly)* Oh, you know what else?

Leader: What?

Schooner: *(speaking faster and faster.)* He told me about a new parrot treat called Zowie. It comes in three different seeds, shelled and unshelled, with bits of fruit. It's an energy treat that gives you lots of pep and, *squawk*, it does!

Leader: How many treats have you had, Schooner?

Schooner: Seven.

Leader: *(nodding)* I thought so. Sam must be a good friend.

Schooner: I think so too.

Leader: Why do you think he shares with you all that good stuff?

Schooner: We like each other.

Leader: Bingo. And you know good stuff too, Schooner.

Schooner: I do?

Leader: Sure. You know about Jesus, the Son of God.

Schooner: Yep.

Leader: Don't you want your friend to know Jesus?

Schooner: Well, I guess.

Leader: Then tell him! Jesus wants us to tell others all about him.

Schooner: But Sam might think I'm weird.

Leader: How else will he find out about the great news?

Schooner: Hear it on the radio? See it on the Internet?

Leader: Is that how you found out about Jesus?

Schooner: No. You told me, boss.

Leader: Friends share good news.

Schooner: *Squawk.*

Leader: So little bird…

Schooner: I get it, boss. Friends tell friends the good news of Jesus.

Leader: Now you're talking.

Schooner: I've been squawkin' all along. *Squawk!*

Leader: God gives us the power to do his work. With the help of the Holy Spirit we are to witness—tell others—about him. After all, if we don't who will?

Schooner: I'm gonna start today, boss.

Leader: Did anyone ever tell you Schooner that you're the sweetest little bird around?

Schooner: *(shyly)* Aww, boss.

Leader: *(look out to the group)* Bible 4U! and you and you up next!

1 Bible 4U!

Welcome to Bible 4U! Theater! Early one morning you wake up and climb out of bed. Suddenly, you hear your mom shout from the kitchen below, "School's closed! Snow day!" Or you receive an invitation to spend a day at Water World Park. Or you just got word that you won the school raffle and a brand new bike. When we have really good news we want to share it.

Today's story tells us the last instructions of Jesus Christ before he went into heaven. This is how the Bible book of Acts opens. That's a pretty suspenseful beginning, don't you think? How can it get any better?

Instant Prep
Pick two reporters and two witnesses. Give each person a copy of "Good News!" script to review.

for Overachievers
Have a drama team prepare the story. Dress reporters in dress up clothes and hats, with pencils, notebooks, tape recorder, camera. The witnesses can wear Bibletime clothes and sandals. Make a backdrop of a Bibletime town.

It does! Jesus gave his disciples a job to do that still applies to us today. And he promised them a gift that would help them carry out the job.

The rest of the Book of Acts is how the disciples followed Jesus' instructions, so we have a lot of great stories ahead of us, and a lot of wonderful examples to follow.

I see a couple of reporters ready to interview eyewitnesses to get the scoop on today's Bible story. Let's investigate.

Good News!
Based on Acts 1:1-11

Reporters enter.

Reporter 1: Hi, everyone. I'm Katie Curious, a news reporter for the Jerusalem Daily Trumpet. We're here to ferret out the facts about what happened in the town of Jerusalem earlier today.

Reporter 2: *(smiles broadly)* I'm Philip the famous photographer, here to help. There's a real buzz going on, something about Jesus and angels.

Reporter 1: Everywhere Jesus goes he's big news. Let's see if we can find out what happened. They said he was here earlier, but I don't see him anywhere. *(looks around)*

Jeremiah, a witness, enters as if in a hurry.

Reporter 2: Sir! Can you stop a minute? We need answers to a few questions. We heard Jesus was here earlier. Can you tell us what happened today? *(snaps a picture)*

Jeremiah: Sure, I was here. It...it...it was the most amazing thing. You won't believe me.

Reporter 1: We'd like to get it in the newspaper for others to read.

Jeremiah: Well, where do I start? It's all amazing. Remember, Jesus was killed on the cross, and then he became alive again. Alive! For the last 40 days he's been popping up all over the place talking to his followers about the kingdom of God. We never knew when to expect him.

Reporter 2: *(checks notebook)* Yes, I believe we have that information. What else can you tell us?

Jeremiah: Today his disciples got together. You know, having a nice meal, taking a break. Jesus joined them and talked about how his cousin John baptized people with water but the Holy Spirit will baptize us!

Reporter 1: What did you think that meant?

Jeremiah: Some in the room thought that Jesus was ready to establish the kingdom of God right then and there.

Reporter 2: And was he?

Jeremiah: *(shakes his head)* No.

Reporter 1: No?

Jeremiah: Jesus said his Father in heaven would bring the kingdom in his good time.

Reporter 2: I still don't understand.

Jeremiah: Hey, I'm sorry, but I've got to go. I don't want to miss out on the baptism of the Holy Spirit.

Jeremiah exits. Mary enters.

Reporter 2: Excuse me, ma'am. Can we ask you a few questions?

Mary: If it doesn't take too long.

Reporter 1: Jesus said everyone should wait to be baptized by the Holy Spirit. Were there any other last minute instructions?

Mary: Yes. He said we were to tell others all about him. Not just Jerusalem. Jesus really meant the whole world!

Reporter 2: Well, we'll put the good news in the paper. We wanted to get an interview with Jesus Christ himself. But we can't find him.

Mary: He's not here.

Reporter 1: Do you know where we can find him?

Mary: *(looks up)* I don't think you're going to get that interview.

Reporter 2: *(snaps a picture)* If you just tell us where he went, we'll catch up with him.

Mary: I don't think you understand. He rose. His body went up above the treetops until he disappeared into the clouds.

Reporter 1: Clouds? *(looks up)*

Mary: Gone. Just like that. I stood there watching the sky, when suddenly two men appeared dressed in white so bright that it hurt my eyes.

Reporter 1: Really? What did they say? *(grabs pencil ready to write)*

Mary: The angels said someday Jesus would come back the same way he left. Then, poof, they were gone, too.

Reporter 2: *(holding up camera)* Can you point up to the sky while I get your picture?

Mary: *(poses)* Hurry, please. I want to get back to the group waiting for the Holy Spirit. I'll spend my life following Jesus and telling everyone the good news.

Reporter 2: *(snaps a picture)* I don't get it. What is the good news?

Mary: Haven't you heard? God loved the world so much that he sent Jesus, his only Son, into our world. Anyone who believes in him will live forever with him in heaven. God sent Jesus Christ to save the world. We don't have to live in the darkness of sin anymore. Jesus is the light of the world.

Reporter 1: *(reflects)* Hmm. Jesus: The Light of the World. I think we have our headline!

Reporters exit discussing the good news.

Bible 4U!

Before Jesus went to heaven and disappeared from the sight of his followers he said, "Go into all the world and preach the gospel." Jesus wants us to spread the good news throughout the world. How much good news do you remember from today's Ascension story?

Toss the four numbered balls to different parts of the room. Bring kids with the balls to the front one-by-one and ask these questions. Allow kids to get help from the group if they need it. After each correct answer, let kids drop the ball into a bag.

 ■ Jesus told his followers to go out into the world. What was their assignment?

 ■ What did Jesus tell the disciples about baptism?

 ■ How did Jesus leave the disciples? How do you think they reacted?

 ■ Who told the disciples to stop staring at the sky?

People need to hear about the hope God offers today. As Christians, we get to help spread light in the darkness of our sin-filled world. That light is Jesus Christ. The instructions that Jesus gave the disciples that day are for us to follow as well. If we believe in Jesus, we're disciples, and Jesus wants us to help other people become disciples too. Jesus told the original disciples to go and tell others of the good news in Jerusalem and spread out from there. We can start where we are, too, by talking to our family, friends and neighbors.

After all, it's such good news we just can't keep it to ourselves!

Someday God may send us to a foreign country to spread the good news. Wherever we are, the Holy Spirit, our helper who lives within us will know what to say and what to do. We do what Jesus asks us to do by the power of the Holy Spirit. Let's remember to trust in him.

Bible Verse
"You will be my witnesses in Jerusalem, and in all Judea and Samaria, and to the ends of the earth." Acts 1:8

Today in your shepherd groups, you'll learn more about spreading the Good News.

Dismiss kids to their shepherd groups.

② Shepherd's Spot

Gather your small group and help kids find Acts 1:1–11 in their Bibles. Have volunteers take turns reading parts of Acts 1:1–11 aloud.

■ **Jesus used only a few words to tell his followers a very important message. What final instructions did Jesus give those who had gathered to hear him speak?**

■ **When you spread Jesus' message of love and hope, what words will you use? Jesus promised to help us. How can the power of the Holy Spirit help when you can't find the words?**

Pass out the "Jerusalem Daily Trumpet" handout. Have kids fill in their names on the Managing Editor line. Look up John 8:12 together and fill in the blanks of the verse. Invite kids to draw in the For Sale box something that might have been for sale in Bible times. For example, clay pots, clay water jars, sheep, wool, baked bread, sandals, bottles of perfumed oil, jewelry, etc.

Have a volunteer read the Jesus Disappears! article from the handout, ending with Acts 1:8: "You will be my witnesses in Jerusalem, and in all Judea and Samaria, and to the ends of the earth."

■ **Jesus could have taken a walk into the hills where no one would have seen him rise into the clouds. Why do you think Jesus wanted his followers to see his display of power?**

■ **You're sitting next to Jesus at suppertime. Suddenly, with no words of explanation he stands and rises into heaven. What might have been your reaction? What would you have told your friends the next day?**

Jesus told us to tell people everywhere that God loves and forgives them. God is counting on you to speak to someone who has no one else to tell him or her about his love. Let's pray for people who need to hear about the hope and light God's love can bring to sad and hopeless hearts. Invite kids to share prayer concerns. **Dear Lord, please help us share your message of light and love with people who are in darkness. We especially pray for _____.** Pause for kids to mention names. **Thank you for giving us the Holy Spirit to help us tell others about you. In Jesus' name, amen.**

Have kids roll up their newspapers as scrolls to take home. Provide ribbon or twine for securing.

Jerusalem Daily Trumpet

_____, Managing Editor

JESUS DISAPPEARS!

ACCORDING TO several hundred witnesses, just forty days after overcoming death, Jesus ascended to heaven, disappearing into the clouds. News has it that during these forty days, Jesus had appeared to his followers many times, proving that he was alive. Today's ascension, however, leaves his followers stunned. They stared at the sky intently until two angels assured them Jesus would return one day.

In the meantime, Jesus' followers are anxious to follow his final instructions to wait in Jerusalem for the Holy Spirit to come, then to go to the whole world with the good news of Jesus.

In his final words, Jesus said, "You will be my witnesses in Jerusalem, and in all Judea and Samaria, and to the ends of the earth" (Acts 1:8).

MORE GOOD NEWS

Jesus said, "I am the _____ of the _____. Whoever follows me will never walk in _____, but will have the _____ of _____"

(John 8:12).

For Sale

MORE GOOD NEWS!

For God so loved the world that he gave his one and only Son, that whoever believes in him shall not perish but have eternal life.   John 3:16

Workshop Wonders*

Set out the supplies and food to make "Ascension" fruit cups.

Distribute the foam cups, one per child. **Imagine you are a boy or girl in biblical times. With your family you saw Jesus die on the cross and buried. You remember feeling sad and confused. But now Jesus is standing beside you. You can ask him questions and hear his voice as he answers. You can touch his hands, sit in his lap, and look into his eyes. He tells you that you are to tell others about him. About his goodness, love and mercy. Then Jesus vanishes. He goes away again, but this time you watch him rise into the sky, and disappear into the clouds. This time you are not sad. You are much too surprised to be sad!**

Get List:
- ❏ foam cups
- ❏ straws
- ❏ scissors
- ❏ spray whipped cream
- ❏ grapes and strawberry pieces
- ❏ plastic knives
- ❏ plastic spoons
- ❏ paper towels

■ **You can never be the same once you invite Jesus into your heart. What are your plans after church today? How will your helper the Holy Spirit guide you to share Jesus' love with others?**

■ **Jesus did not need to pull out a map to find his way to heaven. He had no false starts or second guesses. How does this help you trust God with all your heart?**

Even though you and I weren't with the disciples when Jesus rose into heaven, God wants us to tell the story to others. I have a fun way for us to eat a delicious fruit snack and it will help you retell today's rise up Ascension story to your friends and family.

Use knives to cut away an arch or oval section from the side of the cups leaving the bottom of the cup intact. Snip the end of a straw to sharpen it and stick the point through a fruit piece. Spray the top of the cups with whipped cream.

Now comes the fun way to eat our fruit. Put your straw through the open side of the cup and push it up in and through the whipped cream "clouds." Take a bite of fruit. For each bite, pull the straw out and place a new piece of fruit on the tip, then push it up through the clouds again.

Option: If you prefer, turn the cup over and poke a hole through the cup's bottom. Push the straw through. Place fruit on the straw from within the cup and push it up through the whipped cream.

*Check with parents for any allergies children may have.

Fold down the corners to
start your paper airplane.

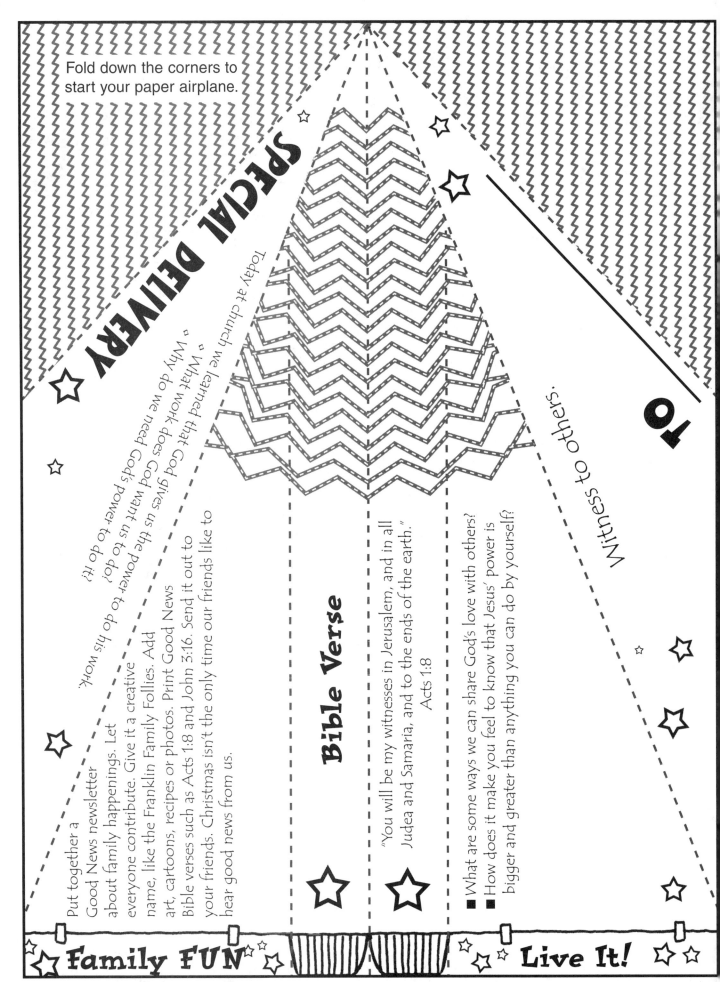

SPECIAL DELIVERY

TO

Witness to others.

Today at church we learned that God gives us the power to do his work. "What work does God want us to do? "Why do we need God's power to do it?

Put together a Good News newsletter about family happenings. Let everyone contribute. Give it a creative name, like the Franklin Family Follies. Add art, cartoons, recipes or photos. Print Good News Bible verses such as Acts 1:8 and John 3:16. Send it out to your friends. Christmas isn't the only time our friends like to hear good news from us.

Bible Verse

"You will be my witnesses in Jerusalem, and in all Judea and Samaria, and to the ends of the earth."
Acts 1:8

■ What are some ways we can share God's love with others?
■ How does it make you feel to know that Jesus' power is bigger and greater than anything you can do by yourself?

☆ Family FUN ☆ ☆ Live It! ☆

Spirit Fire

Option

Get Set
LARGE GROUP ■ Greet kids and do a puppet skit. Schooner asks lots of questions to uncover a mystery gift.
❏ large bird puppet ❏ puppeteer

1

Bible 4U! Instant Drama
LARGE GROUP ■ The apostle Luke explains his research for his biblical account of Pentecost.
❏ 9 actors ❏ copies of pp. 20–21, "Tongues of Fire" script ❏ 4 numbered balls
Optional: ❏ Bibletime costumes ❏ medical scrubs and stethoscope
❏ Bible ❏ pencil ❏ paper plates or fans or electric fan

2

Shepherd's Spot
SMALL GROUP ■ Use the "Holy Spirit Fire" handout to encourage kids to speak to others about God's love. Share concerns and pray together. Send home the Special Delivery handout.
❏ Bibles ❏ pencils ❏ scissors ❏ copies of p. 24, "Holy Spirit Fire"
❏ copies of p. 26, Special Delivery

Option

Workshop Wonders
SMALL GROUP ■ Bright paint and straws help make a "flaming" craft for today's Pentecost story.
❏ pencils ❏ newspaper ❏ red and white construction paper ❏ red, yellow, and orange paint, thinned with water ❏ plastic spoons ❏ straws ❏ stapler

Bible Basis
The Holy Spirit comes at Pentecost. Acts 2:1–12, 22–24, 38–39, 41

Learn It!
The Holy Spirit is God's gift to us.

Live It!
Be faithful disciples.

Bible Verse
"I will ask the Father, and he will give you another Counselor to be with you forever—the Spirit of truth." John 14:16–17

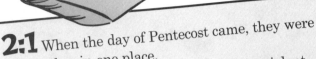

Quick Takes

2:1 When the day of Pentecost came, they were all together in one place.

2 Suddenly a sound like the blowing of a violent wind came from heaven and filled the whole house where they were sitting.

3 They saw what seemed to be tongues of fire that separated and came to rest on each of them.

4 All of them were filled with the Holy Spirit and began to speak in other tongues as the Spirit enabled them.

5 Now there were staying in Jerusalem God-fearing Jews from every nation under heaven.

6 When they heard this sound, a crowd came together in bewilderment, because each one heard them speaking in his own language.

7 Utterly amazed, they asked: "Are not all these men who are speaking Galileans?

8 "Then how is it that each of us hears them in his own native language?

9 "Parthians, Medes and Elamites; residents of Mesopotamia, Judea and Cappadocia, Pontus and Asia,

10 "Phrygia and Pamphylia, Egypt and the parts of Libya near Cyrene; visitors from Rome

11 (both Jews and converts to Judaism); Cretans and Arabs—we hear them declaring the wonders of God in our own tongues!"

12 Amazed and perplexed, they asked one another, "What does this mean?"

22 "Men of Israel, listen to this: Jesus of Nazareth was a man accredited by God to you by miracles, wonders and signs, which God did among you through him, as you yourselves know.

23 "This man was handed over to you by God's set purpose and foreknowledge; and you, with the help of wicked men, put him to death by nailing him to the cross."

24 "But God raised him from the dead, freeing him from the agony of death, because it was impossible for death to keep its hold on him."

38 Peter replied, "Repent and be baptized, every one of you, in the name of Jesus Christ for the forgiveness of your sins. And you will receive the gift of the Holy Spirit.

39 "The promise is for you and your children and for all who are far off—for all whom the Lord our God will call."

41 Those who accepted his message were baptized, and about three thousand were added to their number that day.

Insights

Jesus had ascended into heaven and his followers were staying in Jerusalem as he instructed them to do. He told them to wait for the gift of the Holy Spirit of God. Thousands of Jews were gathered in the city for the celebration of the Feast of Pentecost, which occurred 50 days after Passover. They had come from many different nations and spoke many languages. Some came over the great roads the Romans had built to move their armies around. Others came by boat.

Peter and the other dedicated followers of Jesus (about 120 people) had a good opportunity with a big 'but.' If they could tell these Jews from other countries about Jesus, they in turn would tell others. The people could go back to their countries and share the Good News. But the disciples couldn't speak the languages of the visitors. As usual, God had plans.

A violent wind is an Old Testament symbol of the Spirit of God. When a powerful wind blew through the place where the disciples were meeting, they knew what it meant. The Holy Spirit Jesus had promised had come. The surprise was what the Spirit enabled them to do—speak dozens of languages they had never studied. Everyone present heard the gospel, no matter what language they spoke. Approximately 3,000 people repented of their sins, were baptized and became followers of Christ that day.

Be encouraged as you teach young people; God's power overcomes all obstacles and our human weaknesses. You are planting seeds of faith. Ask the Holy Spirit to enable you to speak the heart language of children. Teach them that they are not alone, because God gave them a loving Counselor; the Holy Spirit.

Get Set

Today let's talk presents. Birthday presents. Holiday presents. Just-because-I-love-you-presents. If you love presents wiggle your left ear. *Pause for kids to try and respond!* **The ones I like the best are the presents that come as a surprise.** *Schooner pops up.*

Schooner: Presents? For me? Did I hear you say a present for me?

Leader: Schooner, hello.

Schooner: Hi, boss. Present? A gift wrapped in glitter paper? For me? *(wiggles excitedly)*

Leader: You really do like gifts!

Schooner: Can you think of anything better?

Leader: Gifts are fun.

Schooner: Oooh, yeah. And when you shake the box, it makes that *ch-ch-ch* sound.

Leader: What sound?

Schooner: You know, the sound that says, "Guess what I am."

Leader: Oh, yes, that sound.

Schooner: And the suspense! Oooh, the suspense! I can hardly stand it! Present? Gift? Me!

Leader: Schooner, you're ready to take off!

Schooner: Don't *you* get excited about presents, boss?

Leader: I suppose I do.

Schooner: What's your favorite part?

Leader: Favorite part?

Schooner: You know. The pretty paper? The ribbon? The shaking?

Leader: Oh, I see. I suppose I like the waiting.

Schooner: The waiting?

Leader: Yes, the waiting.

Schooner: You gotta be kidding, boss. *Squawk!*

Leader: I get a warm feeling inside just knowing that someone loves me enough to give me a gift. For me, it's better than opening the present. It's the way I feel about the gifts of God too.

Schooner: God gives gifts?

Leader: Sure. In fact, today's Bible story is about one of God's gifts.

Schooner: Was it wrapped up?

Leader: Wrapped in fire!

Schooner: You're kidding?

Leader: Not at all. The disciples knew something was coming because Jesus had told them to wait for it. This gift is also for all who follow Jesus.

Schooner: Present! Gift! Glitter paper! Me!

Leader: It's a special gift for everyone here.

Schooner: Tell me already! What is it? *Squawk! (ruffles feathers)*

Leader: Patience, Schooner.

Schooner: *Patience!* That's the gift?!

Leader: The present was the Holy Spirit.

Schooner: Holy Spirit?

Leader: Yes, God sent what seemed like a mighty rushing wind and believers were suddenly filled with the energy and power of the Holy Spirit. The Holy Spirit is our helper. The Holy Spirit helps us do God's will on earth.

Schooner: Oh my. I'm overwhelmed, boss. God's spirit is in me!

Leader: Tongues of fire appeared near the disciples' heads.

Schooner: Majorly spectacular! *Squawk!*

Leader: It just happens that Jews from all over the world were in Jerusalem that day. When they heard the excitement they rushed to the room where the believers sat and heard everything in their own languages.

Schooner: There should be a name for that kinda day.

Leader: We remember the day as Pentecost.

Schooner: Let's have a Pentecost party! Presents. Gifts. Glitter paper. Me!

Leader: We can think of the Holy Spirit as a "just-because-I-love you" gift from our Creator. God gives us everything we need. After our Bible 4U! we can do a little celebrating, Schooner.

Schooner: All I need is a reason and a season—and a little room to flap my tail feathers. Woo-hoo!

1 Bible 4U!

Jesus had ascended into heaven and his followers were staying in Jerusalem as he instructed them to do. He told them to wait. Something was coming. Something just for them. Wait. It's coming. Not in their wildest dreams, however, could they have prepared themselves for the overwhelming gift to come. In his mighty wisdom God would send a piece of himself, the invisible yet powerful Holy Spirit.

Instant Prep
Select an excellent reader to be Luke, or play him yourself. Choose confident readers to play Amal, Jerusha, Micah and Peter and give everyone a copy of the "Tongues of Fire" script, a Bible, pencil, fans.

A violent wind is an Old Testament symbol of the Spirit of God. The Spirit enabled Jesus followers to speak many languages they had never studied. Everyone present heard the word of Peter and the gospel no matter what language they spoke. Three thousand people repented of their sins, were baptized and became followers of Christ that day.

for Overachievers
Have a drama team prepare the story. Dress in Bibletime costumes except for Luke who wears medical garb and a stethoscope. Prepare a backdrop of a city, with a house with a table and chairs in the foreground. Rehearse the special effects with your crew, a Bible, pencil, fans, or electric fan.

Pass out fans (or use paper plate fans). With your kids, practice making a roaring wind with whistle sound effects. On cue, have kids produce the violent wind in today's Bible drama.

Tongues of Fire
Based on Acts 2:1–12, 22–24, 38–39, 41

Luke: *(Bible and pencil in hand)* My name is Luke. I'm a doctor, and a disciple of Jesus Christ. I wrote the Book of Luke in your Bible and about the life of Jesus while he lived on earth. Maybe you've read it. Raise your hand if you've heard of me.

Luke pauses to acknowledge raised hands.

Luke: I'm working on another book. I'll name this book Acts, because of the miraculous acts of God and Jesus' followers since he left earth. If you listen carefully, I'll let you in

on some of my research. It all started at the Feast of Pentecost. Thousands of Jews came from all over the world to Jerusalem to celebrate "The Feast of Weeks." Here's what I heard when I visited with one family, Amal, Jerusha, and Micah.

Luke pretends to write in his Bible while actors speak.

Amal: How exciting, my children! To be in Jerusalem, the City of David, to celebrate the Feast of Pentecost! It was a long tiring trip, on the Roman roads.

Jerusha: I wish we could come here every year to celebrate! Look at all the people.

Amal: They come from all over the world for the feast.

Jerusha: There must be thousands! How many places are they from?

Amal: Let's see, there are the Parthians, the Medes and the Elamites.

Micah: The who?

Amal: And the people from Mesopotamia, Judea and Cappadocia.

Micah: Cappado-who?

Amal: And then there's Pontus, and Asia, Phrygia and Pamphylia, Egypt, and parts of Libya.

Jerusha: I don't even know where some of those places are.

Amal: And we can't forget Rome.

Jerusha: (sighs) Too many places to count.

Micah: I like to see the people. But they talk funny. I can't understand them.

Amal: That's because they are from different countries with different languages.

Micah: Maybe we need to hire a translator. You know, someone who speaks our language.

Jerusha: Can I buy a Jerusalem charm for my bracelet to remember this special trip?

Micah: I want to get one of those orange T-shirts that says City of David with a picture of him killing the giant on the back of it.

Amal: There will be plenty of time for shopping later, children. We need to find a place to stay. I wish your mother could have come, but it would have been too hard for her with the new baby.

Amal, Jerusha, and Micah freeze. Peter joins them.

Luke: (looks up from his writing) In the middle of this big Feast, Jesus' followers were meeting in a house. Amal, Jerusha, and Micah were there, so I asked them to tell me what they saw and heard.

Leader gives signal for wind and roar. Leader gives stop signal.

Amal: (hands over ears) What was that sound? I've never heard a wind like that. It hurt my ears!

Jerusha: Did you see the fire on their heads? Where did that come from?

Micah: Hey! I can understand that guy now. He's speaking our language!

Amal: Galileans are all talking in different languages. How can this be? They are ordinary men and women, not scholars who study languages.

Peter: Listen, everyone! I am Peter, a follower of Jesus Christ. Let me explain what has happened. God's Holy Spirit gave us your languages so we can tell you the good news.

Micah: What good news is he talking about?

Peter: Jesus taught and did many miracles among you, but he was put to death on a cross. God raised Jesus from the dead and made him Lord and Christ. Jesus is the Messiah we have all waited for.

Amal: The Messiah? Here at last!

Jerusha: This sounds like big stuff! We have to remember to tell Mom.

Peter: Be sorry and turn from the wrong you have done. Be baptized into new life with Jesus Christ. You and all your families will receive God's Holy Spirit.

Amal: My family and I want to follow Jesus Christ. Come, children. Let's be baptized to show our new faith. Then we'll go home and tell everyone we know this good news about Jesus Christ.

Peter, Amal, Jerusha, and Micah exit.

Luke: (stops writing and gently closes the Bible) On that day nearly 3,000 people believed in Jesus and were baptized. They began learning more about Jesus and all the things he did. They received the gift of the Holy Spirit. They learned how people who believe in Christ should live and act toward others. The word of Jesus spread all over the world. I lived a long way from Jerusalem, but when I heard the news, I believed too. Read my book, the Book of Acts, and learn more of the amazing power of Jesus.

Luke exits.

God's heart forgives those who are sorry for the wrong they have done. We have good news of God's love that people everywhere need to hear. The Holy Spirit helps us share the good news about Jesus. Let's see what you remember from today's story.

Toss the four numbered balls to different parts of the room. Bring kids with the balls to the front one-by-one and ask these questions. Allow kids to get help from the group if they need it. After each correct answer, let kids drop the ball into a bag.

■ **What force of nature raced through the house where the disciples met?**

■ **What gift did God give that day that we enjoy as well?**

■ **Why was it important that the disciples speak in languages understood in far away lands?**

■ **God cares for all people. Even unbelievers. What in today's story tells us that?**

On the day of Pentecost, Peter, the disciples, and all the new Christians who witnessed the Holy Spirit's power changed in a forever-kind-of-way. They could no longer deny the voice of God inside and return to their sinful lives. The Holy Spirit now flamed within them. Their new on fire hearts grew in love and they followed it. Read aloud two verses from today's Scripture, Acts 2:22–24.

"Men of Israel, listen to this: Jesus of Nazareth was a man accredited by God to you by miracles, wonders and signs, which God did among you through him, as you yourselves know.

This man was handed over to you by God's set purpose and foreknowledge; and you, with the help of wicked men, put him to death by nailing him to the cross.

But God raised him from the dead, freeing him from the agony of death, because it was impossible for death to keep its hold on him."

When Jesus lived on earth he had power over the natural world. Yet, Jesus' power was not confined just to the world of man. His power controls heaven and earth. The Holy Spirit Jesus promised to the believers is the same Holy Spirit we have to help us today. Today in your shepherd groups, you'll talk about the special gift and power of the Holy Spirit and ways you can be faithful disciples too.

Bible Verse
"I will ask the Father, and he will give you another Counselor to be with you forever—the Spirit of truth." John 14:16–17

Dismiss kids to their shepherd groups.

22

② Shepherd's Spot

Gather your small group and help kids find Acts 2 and John 14:16–17 in their Bibles. Ask a volunteer to read John 14:16–17 aloud: "I will ask the Father, and he will give you another Counselor to be with you forever—the Spirit of truth."

Even though Jesus was no longer physically with his followers, he told them he would send them a helper and comforter. We know this helper to be the Holy Spirit. How wonderful that they listened and waited and did not take a vacation or pack up and move away. What they would have missed! God asks that we continue to worship him as we wait for his help and powerful ways.

Review the highlights of the Bible story or have volunteers take turns reading the Bible verses aloud (Acts 2:1–12, 22–24, 38–39, 41).

- **What power words would you use to describe the Holy Spirit?**
- **Did the followers of Jesus have any doubt that the Holy Spirit had come? How did the Holy Spirit make his presence known?**

A warm and welcoming campfire is wonderful on a chilly summer night. A campfire's flames are bright enough to read by. The next time you experience a campfire think of the brightness and warmth of the Holy Spirit. The next time you see the flicker of church candles or the golden glow of birthday candles think of the flames that appeared at Pentecost.

Pass out the "Holy Spirit Fire" handout. Have kids cut out and assemble the campfire stand according the instructions on the handout. As they do, review today's Learn It! and Live It!.

Learn It! The Holy Spirit is God's gift to us.
Live It! Be faithful disciples.

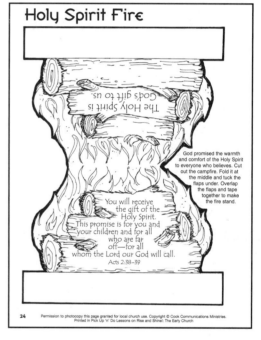

Holy Spirit Fire

The Holy Spirit is God's gift to us.

God promised the warmth and comfort of the Holy Spirit to everyone who believes. Cut out the campfire. Fold it at the middle and tuck the flaps under. Overlap the flaps and tape together to make the fire stand.

You will receive the gift of the Holy Spirit. This promise is for you and your children and for all who are far off—for all whom the Lord our God will call. Acts 2:38–39

24 Permission to photocopy this page granted for local church use. Copyright © Cook Communications Ministries. Printed in Pick Up 'n' Do Lessons on Rise and Shine!: The Early Church

Let's pray for people who need the light and warmth of God's love. Invite kids to share prayer concerns, then pray together. **Dear Lord, give us Holy Spirit fire to share your message of light and love with people who are in darkness. We pray for people who don't know you.** Pause to invite kids to say names. **Please give us courage to share about you and strength to love others and be a warm light wherever we go this week. Thank you for the gift of your Holy Spirit. In Jesus' name, amen."**

Holy Spirit Fire

The Holy Spirit is God's gift to us.

God promised the warmth and comfort of the Holy Spirit to everyone who believes. Cut out the campfire. Fold it at the middle and tuck the flaps under. Overlap the flaps and tape together to make the fire stand.

You will receive the gift of the Holy Spirit. This promise is for you and your children and for all who are far off—for all whom the Lord our God will call.
Acts 2:38–39

Workshop Wonders

For this craft, cut the white construction paper slightly smaller than the red. The red paper will form a frame for the white one. Trim the paper ahead of time or have kids do it before beginning the project. Cover tables with newspapers and set out paint, spoons and straws.

Ask kids to draw three or four figures on their papers to represent the followers in today's story. Print today's Bible verse near the bottom.

"I will ask the Father, and he will give you another Counselor to be with you forever—the Spirit of truth" John 14:16–17.

Get List:
- ❑ pencils
- ❑ newspaper
- ❑ red and white construction paper
- ❑ red, yellow, and orange paint, thinned with water
- ❑ plastic spoons
- ❑ straws
- ❑ stapler

Over 100 followers of Jesus gathered, spending time with each other as Jerusalem celebrated Pentecost. The followers waited and wondered for the gift Jesus promised would come. They weren't sure what to expect, but they trusted Jesus. Then it came. Wham! Just imagine the wind whooshing through your bedroom window like a thunderstorm fast approaching. You just know something powerful is coming! On that day men and woman experienced the power and love of God in a way they could hear and feel. Others could see it too, and people from all over heard Jesus' followers witness about God, each in their own language.

■ **Does knowing the power of God can be seen, felt and heard surprise you? How does it help you trust in him?**

■ **A violent wind or tornado can destroy a house. Yet in today's story, we do not here of anything breaking in the room where the followers gathered. How are all things possible with God?**

Red is the color often used to represent the feast of Pentecost. Let's use a spoon to carefully drip a few drops of red paint onto the white construction paper near the figures you've drawn. A paintbrush will work as well. **Let's liken these drops to the fire that came to rest on the believers in today's story. Now let's drip a little yellow and orange to complete the fiery effect.** Before passing out the straws, use one to demonstrate how to blow gently on the drops to spread the paint into flame-like designs. **As you blow gently, allow the air to push the drops into tongue-like flames as described into today's Bible story. Think about the wind of God. And blow the fire of the Holy Spirit into those that love him!**

Have kids staple their art to the red sheet to frame their artwork.

Fold down the corners to start your paper airplane.

SPECIAL DELIVERY

TO

Today at church we learned that God gave the disciples the Holy Spirit. What's the most amazing thing about how the Holy Spirit came? What would you like the Holy Spirit to do in your life?

Be faithful disciples.

Family FUN

In a darkened room, sit beside a pretend campfire (use bright flashlights covered over with pieces of yellow and red tissue paper. Rubber band the tissue paper in place. Slip your flashlights into narrow baking pans or flowerpots so they stand upright.) As you relax by the fire see how many Bible verses you can recite by memory. No clue? If you get stuck make an effort this week to memorize a Bible verse a day. Look for verses in the Book of Acts or ask mom or dad to help. The Word of God is a lamp to light your way. If you don't know it, even a little, how can it help you or others?

Bible Verse

"I will ask the Father, and he will give you another Counselor to be with you forever—the Spirit of truth." John 14:16-17

Live It!

■ Why is fire a strong symbol of the Holy Spirit? How does it help you to remember the strong, burning Spirit of God?
■ Why should you be a faithful disciple to your friends? (Because it makes you blessed and favored before God. And what could be finer than having God on your side!)

One in Heart and Mind

Option — Get Set
LARGE GROUP ■ Greet kids and do a puppet skit. Schooner finds out just how willing he is to share with others.
❑ large bird puppet ❑ puppeteer

1 — Bible 4U! Instant Drama
LARGE GROUP ■ Sharing in love. Hear all about the devoted members of the early church in today's instant Bible drama.
❑ 5–6 actors ❑ copies of pp. 30-31, "Share and Care" script ❑ 4 numbered balls
Optional: ❑ Bibletime costumes

2 — Shepherd's Spot
SMALL GROUP ■ Use the hand-slapping "Team Spirit" handout to encourage kids to share and work together as a team. Share concerns and pray together. Send home the Special Delivery handout.
❑ Bibles ❑ pencils ❑ scissors ❑ copies of p. 34, "Team Spirit!"
❑ copies of p. 36, Special Delivery

Option — Workshop Wonders *
SMALL GROUP ■ Kids share ingredients to build beautiful edible churches.
❑ bowls ❑ graham crackers or large, flat chocolate cookies or fig cookies
❑ frosting (white, if using chocolate cookies) ❑ cereal in square shapes ❑ soft gumdrops ❑ small colored candy, jellybeans ❑ stick pretzels ❑ plastic knives

*Check with parents for any food allergies children may have.

Bible Basis Devoted believers share. Acts 2:42–47; 4:32–37

Learn It! God wants his people to come together in his name.

Live It! Share freely what you have.

Bible Verse And do not forget to do good and to share with others, for with such sacrifices God is pleased. Hebrews 13:16

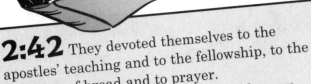

Acts 2:42–47; 4:32–37

2:42 They devoted themselves to the apostles' teaching and to the fellowship, to the breaking of bread and to prayer.
43 Everyone was filled with awe, and many wonders and miraculous signs were done by the apostles.
44 All the believers were together and had everything in common.
45 Selling their possessions and goods, they gave to anyone as he had need.
46 Every day they continued to meet together in the temple courts. They broke bread in their homes and ate together with glad and sincere hearts,
47 praising God and enjoying the favor of all the people. And the Lord added to their number daily those who were being saved.

4:32 All the believers were one in heart and mind. No one claimed that any of his possessions was his own, but they shared everything they had.
33 With great power the apostles continued to testify to the resurrection of the Lord Jesus, and much grace was upon them all.
34 There were no needy persons among them. For from time to time those who owned lands or houses sold them, brought the money from the sales
35 and put it at the apostles' feet, and it was distributed to anyone as he had need.
36 Joseph, a Levite from Cyprus, whom the apostles called Barnabas (which means Son of Encouragement),
37 sold a field he owned and brought the money and put it at the apostles' feet.

Insights

Even though Jesus was no longer physically present with his followers, they followed his teachings, prayed, studied the Scriptures, and enjoyed the encouragement of the Holy Spirit. Acts 4:32 says, "All the believers were one in heart and mind." They shared all their possessions and no one had a need that wasn't met. They met together every day for fellowship. Many miracles occurred because of their faith.

The original 11 disciples (plus Mathias, chosen to replace Judas) led and taught the group. Believers included men and women, rich and poor, scholars and laborers. Everyone used their different gifts and resources for the good of the group. They helped each other and shared everything they had. No one went without things they needed.

These first Christians did not separate themselves from their culture and community. They believed Jesus was the fulfillment of Jewish longing, not a contradiction to it. They continued to worship at the temple and sit under the teaching they received there.

Distinctly Christian practices, such as the Lord's Supper and teaching about Christ, occurred in private homes because of the cultural constrictions. But the Christians showed such enthusiasm and brotherly love that they attracted a steady stream of new believers.

Our consumer society teaches us early on to acquire everything we can. The world encourages us to use people and love things instead of the other way around. In the world we are encouraged to compete to be better, richer, prettier, and the last one standing.

The early Christian model reminds us that God means for his people to be different from the world. We who have been pardoned and given so much should be overflowing with radical gratitude, generosity and grace toward others. Use this lesson to encourage kids to share money, time, and love with others.

Get Set

God loves it when we gather to talk about his Son, Jesus. He's also happy when we work together sharing and caring for each other. Fellowship! It does a world of good. And it was a way of life for the men and women in the early church. Schooner, I'm doing all the talking here. *Schooner pops up.*

Schooner: Yes, boss?

Leader: Hello my friend. I have a question for you.

Schooner: I know it all, boss. *Squawk!*

Leader: If I asked, would you share your sunflower seeds with me?

Schooner: Sure, boss, my pleasure, I'll go get them.

Leader: Just a minute. Would you also share your nibble salt bar and dried fruit?

Schooner: Uh, sure,

Leader: Wonderful.

Schooner: But…wouldn't you rather find your own fruit, boss?

Leader: No, not really. Now would you share your stuffed feather buddy with me?

Schooner: Bobo? But I've had Bobo ever since I was a baby bird!

Leader: I know.

Schooner: Bobo comforts me when I get scared of the dark, and he helped me feel better that time I got the chicken box.

Leader: Chicken pox? I didn't know parrots could get that.

Schooner: Not chicken pox, chicken *box!* Yellow chicks in a cardboard box that my owner got at Easter time. Boy, were they a pain!

Leader: Oh, I see.

Schooner: Kept me up all night with their constant peeping.

Leader: Back to the subject, Schooner. Would you share Bobo?

Schooner: Well, I'll have to think about it. What's all this about, anyway?

Leader: I want to see if you are a World Champion Sharer, like the people in our story today. The men and women of the early church were gold-medal givers.

Schooner: Really?

Leader: Really.

Schooner: What kinds of things did they share?

Leader: The Bible says "everything."

Schooner: No way! Food?

Leader: Yep.

Schooner: Desserts?

Leader: Yep.

Schooner: Homes?

Leader: Yep.

Schooner: Money?

Leader: Yep.

Schooner: Toys?

Leader: Yep.

Schooner: Cuddly comfort toys called Bobo?

Leader: Yep.

Schooner: *(annoyed)* Yep. Yep. Yep. You sound like a baby chick, boss.

Leader: The Bible says that the members of the early church came together, and shared food, clothing and their money. They were happy to be in each other's company.

Schooner: *Squawk!* I need more practice with this sharing thing.

Leader: The Bible says that they were all of one heart, and they didn't consider anything as their own, but shared everything they had.

Schooner: Hmm. I thought if you shared some of your things some of the time you were doing okay.

Leader: God puts people first. Look how he shares his world. And he didn't keep the good stuff for himself either—like pink roses, pretty birds, puppy dogs, or ocean breezes. God's happy when we gather together and share what we have with those who need it.

Schooner: I'd like to learn more about sharing. Will you help me, boss?

Leader: Yep! Bible 4U! up next.

1 Bible 4U!

Welcome to Bible 4U! theater! Today we're going to hear about the first Christians and how God changed their lives. After the Holy Spirit came, Christians shared and helped each other like never before. They learned Jesus' way from his apostles. And they loved each other so much that they wanted to be sure everyone was taken care of. Even people who weren't Christians noticed and more and more decided to follow Jesus.

Even though times are very different now, we can learn a lot from the first Christians. When we follow Jesus and obey God's Word, we share because everything we have is a gift from God. He gives us what we need and wants us to use what we have to share with others. Food, clothing, homes, money, toys. We learn to care more about others than for ourselves. That's the Jesus way. It pleases him to see us share and help others.

The first Christians prayed and met together every day. They were one big family. Let's watch and listen to learn about how the early Christians shared and cared for each other.

Instant Prep

Select three boys and two girls for the roles. You can be the reader or assign the role to an excellent reader. Give your actors copies of "Share and Care" to review.

for Overachievers

Have a drama team prepare the story. Dress everyone in Bibletime costumes. Use a Bibletime city backdrop with painted palm trees and a cardboard donkey.

Share and Care
Based on Acts 2:42–47; 4:32–37

Reader stands to one side of stage.

Reader: After the coming of the Holy Spirit, in the area around Jerusalem, everyone noticed big changes in the people who were called Christians. The believers studied what the apostles taught. They shared life together. They ate bread together, and they prayed together.

Sam and Hadassah enter.

Sam: Man, I don't know what's happened to my friend Ben. He is so different lately. It's like some other person has taken over his body.

Hadassah: That's funny. How is he different?

Sam: He's always running off to a meeting. He says it's teaching and fellowship, and he just can't stay away. And he lets me borrow his donkey for my work any time I want to. He used to always say no, even when I begged.

Hadassah: Hmm. That is different for Ben.

Reader: Everyone felt that God was near. The apostles did miracles. All the believers were together. They shared everything they had. They sold what they owned and gave each other everything they needed.

Hadassah: Come to think of it, my friend Martha has been acting different too. She gave me a whole bag of figs the other day and her secret recipe for fig bars. I could really use the food because my sandal business has been pretty slow lately.

Sam and Hadassah exit. Peter and Ben enter.

Ben: Pete! Hey, big Pete! Can you give me a hand with this load of fish?

Pete: Sure, Ben. Wow! Great catch! These fish will bring in a lot of money at the market. What are you going to do with it all?

Ben: Well, you know that young family with all the little kids? The new Christians? The children could use new tunics and sandals.

Pete: You're giving up your own money to help another family? That's great, Ben!

Pete and Ben exit.
Martha and Hadassah enter.

Reader: Every day they met together in the temple courtyard. In their homes they had dinner together. Their hearts were glad and honest and loyal. They praised God and were respected by all the people.

Martha: Hi, Hadassah. I was just on my way to the temple. Why don't you come along?

Hadassah: *(shrugs)* Okay.

Martha: And after that, maybe you'd like to come with me to a meeting at my house. We'll have a great meal together with some of my other friends.

Hadassah: Well, I guess I could try it.

Martha: *(smiles)* Christians don't bite, you know.

Martha and Hadassah exit. Ben and Sam enter.

Reader: All the believers agreed in heart and mind. They didn't claim that anything they had was their own. With great power the apostles continued their teaching. They gave witness that the Lord Jesus had risen from the dead. And they were greatly blessed by God.

Sam: I don't get it, Ben. I really appreciate that you let me use your donkey. But why are you being so nice?

Ben: I made a new friend in Jesus.

Sam: That man who was crucified?

Ben: That's the one. He came back to life, you know.

Sam: I heard that rumor. I don't believe it.

Ben: It's not a rumor. It's true. And once you get to know him, you'll understand why I'm a changed man.

Sam: Maybe you should tell me more about this Jesus.

Reader: There were no needy persons among them. For from time to time those who owned lands or houses sold them, brought the money from the sales and put it at the apostles' feet, and it was given out to anyone who needed it.

Ben: I'll tell you everything you want to know about Jesus. And I'd like you to meet a friend of mine. His name is Barnabas.

Reader: Joseph was a Levite from Cyprus. The apostles called him Barnabas. The name Barnabas means Son of Encouragement. He sold a field he owned and gave the money to the apostles.

Sam and Ben exit. Sam returns, this time with Hadassah.

Hadassah: Sam! My friend Martha invited me to a meal at her house. *(rubs stomach)* Lamb stew. It really hit the spot!

Sam: Ben introduced me to his friend Barnabas, and I ate with them.

Hadassah: These Christians are all right. They still go to the temple and worship God and listen to the teaching. But they take their religion personally.

Sam: I know. Ben is a changed man. If knowing Jesus can change someone as selfish as Ben, there must be something to it.

Hadassah: You know, I think I'm going to look into this more. Caring and sharing sounds like a great way to live!

Reader: Every day the Lord added to their group those who were being saved.

Sam and Hadassah exit.

When we understand that everything we have comes from God then we are thankful for what he's given us. In turn we can be generous with our things. Sharing comes from a grateful heart. Let's see who can share a few answers about our story with the group today. Heads up. Here come the balls!

Toss the four numbered balls to different parts of the room. Bring kids with the balls to the front one-by-one and ask these questions. Allow kids to get help from the group if they need it. After each correct answer, let kids drop the ball into a bag.

 ■ What change did Sam and Hadassah notice in their Christian friends? How were their actions different from before?

 ■ Name three things the early Christians did together in fellowship?

 ■ What does the phrase "one in heart and mind" mean to you?

 ■ Name two things of value the Christians sold so that "there were no needy persons among them"? Acts 4:34

Becoming Christians changes us from the inside out. Sharing doesn't come naturally to most of us. Often, we tune out what others teach us about sharing. We do things our own way and use words like "me" and "mine." But God wants his people to come together in his name to do his work. His Spirit living in us changes everything. We work for God now!

When we become Christians we are on the same team. We work together, have fun together, share generously and welcome others. The first Christians did not separate themselves from their neighbors who were unbelievers. But they learned all they could about the risen Jesus from the apostles who knew him well. The enthusiasm and brotherly love of the early church attracted many new believers.

> **Bible Verse**
> And do not forget to do good and to share with others, for with such sacrifices God is pleased. Hebrews 13:16

When we ask Jesus to be our Savior, he begins to change us to be more like him. Then, just like in our story, other people notice how we treat others and are curious about Jesus. When Christians work together, caring and sharing together like a team, people notice. Today in your shepherd groups, you'll learn about having a Christian team spirit.

Dismiss kids to their shepherd groups.

② Shepherd's Spot

Gather your small group and help kids find Acts 2:42–47 and 4:32–37 in their Bibles.

Belief in Jesus Christ changes who we are. When the early believers committed to Jesus, their lives—and how they did things—changed radically. They spent time listening to the teaching ways of Jesus, and they prayed together. They began sharing as never before—all in joyful team spirit. Go team!

Review the highlights of the Bible story or have volunteers take turns reading Acts 2:42–47 and 4:32–37 aloud.

■ **Name some ways team members on a football or volleyball or soccer team share the outcome of a championship game? Can they win the big game without each other? Do they celebrate as a team?**

■ **How should Christians act toward one another if they are on the same team? How can the Holy Spirit help?**

Pass out the "Team Spirit!" handout. Have kids follow the instructions on the handout to make a unique folding booklet. Instruct kids to write on the hands ideas for ways to share with others, such as food, clothes, time, toys, and so on. Cut out the large shape on the solid lines. Then cut between the sections, being careful not to cut through the fold lines at the center. Fold hand flaps to the center.

Have a volunteer read Hebrews 13:16 from the handout: "And do not forget to do good and to share with others, for with such sacrifices God is pleased."

■ **What is the most valuable thing you own? What would it mean for you to sell it and give the money to the poor?**

■ **Why does sacrifice—doing without so others have what they need—please God?**

■ **Come up with two things that you can share today with a younger brother and sister.**

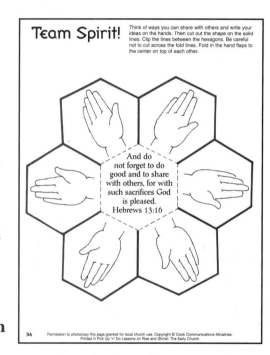

Team Spirit!

Think of ways you can share with others and write your ideas on the hands. Then cut out the shape on the solid lines. Clip the lines between the hexagons. Be careful not to cut across the fold lines. Fold in the hand flaps to the center on top of each other.

And do not forget to do good and to share with others, for with such sacrifices God is pleased. Hebrews 13:16

34 Permission to photocopy this page granted for local church use. Copyright © Cook Communications Ministries.
Printed in Pick Up 'n' Do Lessons on Rise and Shine!: The Early Church

God wants us to share his love and blessings with others. We never need to look far to find people in need. Review today's Learn It! and Live It!.

Learn It! God wants his people to come together in his name.
Live It! Share freely what you have.

Invite kids to share concerns. **Let's pray. Dear Lord, Please give us generous hearts. Give us eyes that see the needs of others. Help us share our bounty and our blessings. We especially pray for the poor in our community who go to bed hungry, who have no homes, who live in temporary shelters, who are sick and need medicine and medical care. In Jesus' name, amen.**

Team Spirit!

Think of ways you can share with others and print your ideas on the hands. Then cut out the shape on the solid lines. Don't forget to cut the lines between the hexagons. But be careful not to cut across the fold lines. Fold in the hand flaps to the center on top of each other.

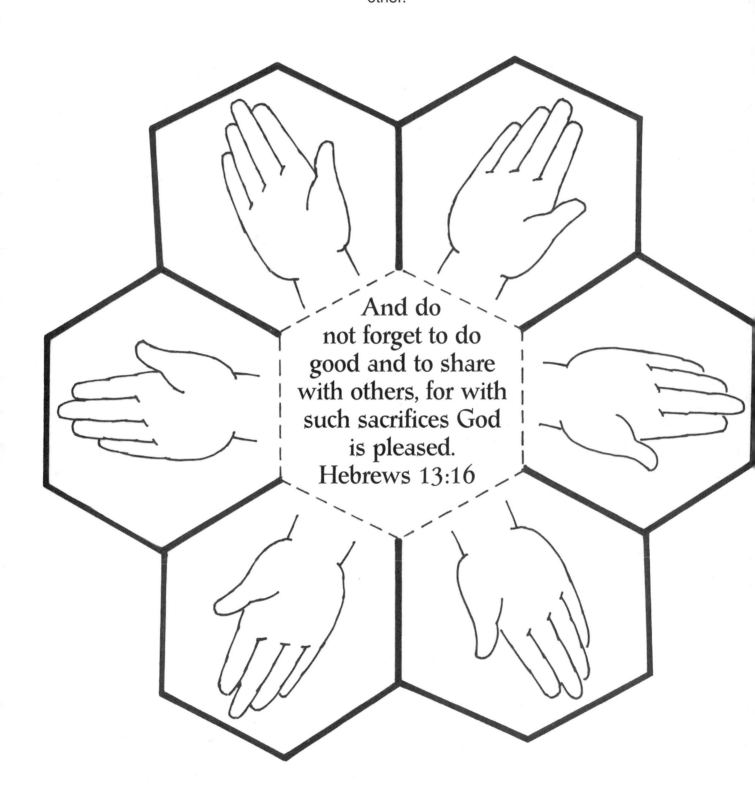

And do not forget to do good and to share with others, for with such sacrifices God is pleased. Hebrews 13:16

Workshop Wonders*

Before class, make a sample edible church for your kids to see. The idea for this snack is not to make a perfect church building but to communicate that the things we treasure most take time and effort. When we share our efforts with others it builds community.

Get List:

- ❏ bowls
- ❏ graham crackers or chocolate or fig cookies
- ❏ white frosting
- ❏ cereal in square shapes
- ❏ soft gumdrops
- ❏ small colored candy, jelly beans
- ❏ stick pretzels
- ❏ plastic knives

The believers in the early church loved to come together and praise God. They knew it made God happy when they did. They knew that God was watching over them. Let's think of our group as a little community of believers.

■ **How does our church share with children in the community?**

God has given us abilities and worldly goods that he wants us to share with others. The people in the early church understood what it meant to depend on each other. They sold their possessions and contributed their money for the use of all. They ate, prayed and worshiped together. We can learn to be good at sharing too.

Set out ingredients in bowls and remind children to share. **Use the treats as building material to make a beautiful church. I'd like you to use your imagination. Your church can be anything you like and not look like anything you've seen before. A church is more than a building. A church is a body of believers who come together to worship God.**

■ **How does it make you feel when you act selfishly with your things? Do you comfort yourself by saying that it's not a big deal? Next time this happens to you, pray and ask for a clean heart. God will forgive your selfishness if you ask him.**

Use the frosting to "cement" the graham crackers or chocolate cookies together. Cookie "towers" can go straight up or cookies can be arranged side-by-side on a plate to make a long row. Cover chocolate cookie rolls with white frosting. Cookie rolls sliced at an angle will reveal fun cream and chocolate stripes. For vertical buildings use soft gumdrops to raise the "floors" of the church. Cut pretzels make great crosses. Use food decorations in any way to enhance the buildings.

Now let's take a look at everyone's churches. Have kids share with the group the idea for their churches. **Good job. They look beautiful!** Enjoy the sweet treat. **And as our verse says, "And do not forget to do good and to share with others, for with such sacrifices God is pleased." Hebrews 13:16**

*Check with parents for any allergies children may have.

Fold down the corners to start your paper airplane.

SPECIAL DELIVERY

TO

Share freely what you have.

Today at church we learned that people in the early church shared everything they had with each other and people in need. • Tell about a time you shared with a friend who forgot her lunch. • Share highlights of today's Bible story.

Family FUN

Serve as a family. Make a list of your family blessings. God gives us things to share with others. Play a game of Monopoly or another game where winning is important. Reverse the rules and see who can give away the most during the game. Talk about ways you can help others close to home and in other countries. Maybe your community has a soup kitchen, children's hospital, nursing home, or another project where your family "team" can help others on a regular basis. Pray to find a need that God puts on your hearts where you can serve others as a family.

Bible Verse

And do not forget to do good and to share with others, for with such sacrifices God is pleased.
Hebrews 13:16

Live It!

- Should you share with others even when they don't share with you? Jesus says, "yes."
- What did Jesus share with his friends before his death on the cross?

Superhero for the Faith

Get Set
Option
LARGE GROUP • ■ Greet kids and do a puppet skit. Schooner listens to the courageous story of the first Christian martyr, Stephen.
❑ large bird puppet ❑ puppeteer

1 Bible 4U! Instant Drama
LARGE GROUP ■ Four actors talk about what is means to be a hero.
❑ 4 actors ❑ copies of pp. 40-41, "A True Hero" script ❑ 4 numbered balls
Optional: ❑ superhero costume or superhero toys

2 Shepherd's Spot
SMALL GROUP ■ Use the "Fearless Faith" handout to encourage kids to speak to others about God's love. Share concerns and pray together. Send home the Special Delivery handout.
❑ Bibles ❑ pencils ❑ scissors ❑ copies of p. 44, "Fearless Faith!"
❑ copies of p. 46, Special Delivery

Workshop Wonders
Option
SMALL GROUP ■ Watch 'em fall! Kids explore the domino effect as they talk about telling others about Jesus.
❑ dominoes ❑ table or uncarpeted floor

Bible Basis
Stephen dies for his faith.
Acts 6:8–15; 7:55—8:1

Learn It!
God is with us when bad things happen.

Live It!
Tell others about Jesus.

Bible Verse
Do not fear, for I am with you; do not be dismayed, for I am your God.
Isaiah 41:10

Quick Takes

Acts 6:8–15; 7:55—8:1

6:8 Now Stephen, a man full of God's grace and power, did great wonders and miraculous signs among the people.
9 Opposition arose, however, from members of the Synagogue of the Freedmen (as it was called)—Jews of Cyrene and Alexandria as well as the provinces of Cilicia and Asia. These men began to argue with Stephen,
10 but they could not stand up against his wisdom or the Spirit by whom he spoke.
11 Then they secretly persuaded some men to say, "We have heard Stephen speak words of blasphemy against Moses and against God."
12 So they stirred up the people and the elders and the teachers of the law. They seized Stephen and brought him before the Sanhedrin.
13 They produced false witnesses, who testified, "This fellow never stops speaking against this holy place and against the law.
14 "For we have heard him say that this Jesus of Nazareth will destroy this place and change the customs Moses handed down to us."
15 All who were sitting in the Sanhedrin looked intently at Stephen, and they saw that his face was like the face of an angel.

7:55 But Stephen, full of the Holy Spirit, looked up to heaven and saw the glory of God, and Jesus standing at the right hand of God.
56 "Look," he said, "I see heaven open and the Son of Man standing at the right hand of God."
57 At this they covered their ears and, yelling at the top of their voices, they all rushed at him,
58 dragged him out of the city and began to stone him. Meanwhile, the witnesses laid their clothes at the feet of a young man named Saul.
59 While they were stoning him, Stephen prayed, "Lord Jesus, receive my spirit."
60 Then he fell on his knees and cried out, "Lord, do not hold this sin against them." When he had said this, he fell asleep.
8:1 And Saul was there, giving approval to his death. On that day a great persecution broke out against the church at Jerusalem, and all except the apostles were scattered throughout Judea and Samaria.

Insights

The word "witness" is mentioned more than 30 times in the Book of Acts. After God sent the Holy Spirit, thousands of people heard and believed the gospel. Faith in Jesus Christ spread like a wildfire with the power of the Holy Spirit. Christians loved to share the good news with everyone they met.

The strictest religious group of this time, the Pharisees, held much power over the Jewish society in Jerusalem. They were fastidious about keeping all the major and minor religious laws of their day. But like some people today, many Pharisees didn't carry their religion into their everyday lives. Instead, they became proud, arrogant, and cruel in punishing anyone in their power who didn't follow all the religious rules. Jesus clashed with them repeatedly. The way they dealt with Stephen was no surprise.

Stephen was one of seven people who supervised food distribution to the needy people in the church. But clearly he was a powerful speaker as well. He was falsely accused by trumped up witnesses. In defending himself, he probably knew he was sealing the decision against him. Still, he spoke boldly and preached the truth of Jesus.

Stephen was a real Christian hero. He was faithful to the end of his life. Children need people to look up to. Some of the children you teach have and will go through difficult seasons in their lives. In one hour a week, you may never see beneath the surface of their lives. But you can arm them with the understanding that God is always with them, especially in difficult times. Use this lesson to encourage kids to trust God and to take a stand for Christ even when it's hard.

Welcome. Today's Bible story is a story on courage. A passionate believer named Stephen gave his life for Jesus Christ. It's a sad story but a real life example on courage for us to learn from. Schooner, let's talk a bit. *Schooner pops up.*

Schooner: *(hangs head)* Boss, today's story is sad.

Leader: *(hugs Schooner)* Yes, it is. But Stephen's story is in the Bible to teach us faithfulness and the courage faith often needs.

Schooner: Why were the people so angry with Stephen, boss?

Leader: Stephen, a man full of God's grace and power, did great wonders and miracles among the people of his day.

Schooner: Well, that's a great thing! Where's the problem?

Leader: The powerful Jewish leaders in Jerusalem wanted religious control. Stephen talked about the power of One, Jesus.

Schooner: Well…did he speak up for himself?

Leader: Yes. But the leaders became angry anyway. They could not stand up against Stephen's wisdom or the Holy Spirit that filled him.

Schooner: Stephen sounds like a real hero, boss.

Leader: Stephen is considered by many believers to be the first martyr for the Christian faith.

Schooner: Mart-er?

Leader: Martyr. A person who gives us his or her life to remain true to Jesus.

Schooner: You know, boss, that's a lot to give up.

Leader: Yes, life is precious. But remember, Schooner, Jesus did that very thing for us. He died on the cross so that our sins would be forgiven and that we could have life forever with him.

Schooner: Hmm.

Leader: Today's story talks about the look on Stephen's face as the crowd screamed insults at him. His face glowed like an angel.

Schooner: Wow.

Leader: Only with the power of the Holy Spirit could Stephen have felt at peace and not overwhelmed by fear.

Schooner: So when we're afraid, we need help to be strong—like Stephen.

Leader: Good point, Schooner.

Schooner: We don't go it alone. We ask for help.

Leader: Absolutely, my little feathered friend.

Schooner: Okay, boss, I'll give it a try.

Leader: When the crowd continued to curse at Stephen and threw more and more stones he prayed for them.

Schooner: *(vexed)* Squawk! What!? Pray for the stone throwers!? No way, boss. That's not what I would have done.

Leader: Followers of Jesus pray for their enemies.

Schooner: But…but…

Leader: No ifs, ands, or buts, Schooner. We are to pray for those who are mean to us.

Schooner: *(shakes head)* This is the toughest lesson of all, boss.

Leaders: I agree. It's not the way we would want to treat our enemies. But it is the way of Jesus.

Schooner: *(ruffles feathers and sits silent.)*

Leader: Schooner, let's not forget, the hope in today's story.

Schooner: What's that, boss?

Leader: God never left Stephen. He was never alone.

Schooner: That helps, boss.

Leader: God gives us courage to tell others about his Son, Jesus, even when others are mean and hurtful.

Schooner: God is a courage-giver. He always makes a way. I love God.

Leader: Me, too, Schooner.

Schooner: *(stretches taller)* I think I'm ready to hear the whole story, boss.

Leader: Bible 4U! Schooner and the rest of us too.

1 Bible 4U!

The early Christians took care of each other, worshiped together, and shared their homes and money with each other. Every day more people became Christians. But not everything that happened was pleasant. Some religious leaders at the time didn't want to see people become Christians. So they shamed and hurt Christians so they would not speak in public. Stephen was a Christian leader. His job was to make sure everybody had food, but he was also a powerful speaker. In order to silence Stephen, religious authorities ended his life.

Instant Prep

Select four people to play the parts of Eric, John, Anna, and Megan. Give each a copy of the "A True Hero" script to review.

for Overachievers

Have a drama team prepare the story. Dress "Eric" in a superhero costume or have him carry superhero toy figures. Use a modern home set with a board game between the actors.

Today's Bible lesson is a serious one. It's about standing up for what you believe. Heroes aren't characters in TV shows or video games or movies. Stephen knew the danger, but still he preached about Jesus. Stephen was a Christian hero who died for his faith. His reward? Eternal life with God the Father and with his Son, Jesus.

Let's listen and learn about the life of a True Hero.

A True Hero
Based on Acts 6:8–15; 7:55—8:1

(Eric enters as his sister and two friends are playing a game.)

Eric: Crash! Bam! Look out! I am Superhero, Mr. Fantastic. I have come to save the world from all evil and from little sisters! Pow! Kaboom!

Anna: Eric! Get out of here! You are such a goof!

Megan: *(rolls eyes)* My brother is the same. He collects Star Wars action figures. He's always saving someone from a cosmic disaster.

Eric: Incoming asteroid! Do not fear. I will destroy it before it destroys the earth! *(strikes superhero pose)*

Anna: Girls can be superheroes, too, you know. I like the idea of being stronger and smarter than anyone else.

Megan: Do ever stop to think about what a real hero is? I mean, a real, true-life hero?

Anna: My aunt is a hero. She serves in the Army.

John: Police officers and firefighters are heroes.

Eric: I once heard about a guy who saved a little girl who fell in the river.

Megan: I was thinking about some of the heroes in the Bible.

John: You mean like Caleb and David and Esther and Daniel?

Megan: Bingo. We have a winner. And Stephen. Stephen was awesome and brave.

Anna: I've heard of Caleb and David and Esther and Daniel. Who was Stephen?

Eric: Yeah, what did he do to be a hero? *(takes various dramatic poses)* Save a village? Fight an army with one hand tied behind his back?

John: Conquer new lands? Save the people from a plague?

Megan: What he did took tremendous courage.

Anna: Are you going to tell us or what?

John: Let's get to the point.

Megan: Stephen wasn't afraid to talk about Jesus.

Eric: That's it? He talked?

Anna: There must be more to the story.

Megan: There is. He was a powerful speaker. When he talked about Jesus, people became Christians.

John: So what's the problem with that? Isn't that what we want?

Megan: Sure, it's what we want. But it's not what the religious leaders of the day wanted.

Eric: Oh, those guys. You're talking about the Pharisees, the ones with all the rules.

Anna: They didn't like Jesus. I bet they didn't like people who talked about him, either.

Megan: Ding, ding! A winning answer! They tried to argue with Stephen, but the Holy Spirit gave Stephen wisdom. They couldn't win the argument.

John: So you're saying he was a hero because he won arguments?

Megan: That's just the beginning.

Eric: Well, what else is there?

Megan: The religious leaders convinced a few people to tell lies about Stephen. They spread rumors that Stephen said Jesus would destroy their town and wreck the Ten Commandments. Big lies like that.

Anna: Did Stephen defend himself?

Megan: It was a set-up from the beginning. Stephen was put on trial, and the witnesses told their lies there.

John: Stephen must have been nervous.

Eric: Not if he was a hero. Pow! Kabloom!

Megan: Stephen was at peace, his face like that of an angel.

Eric: So now what?

Anna: Did he persuade anyone of the power of Jesus?

Megan: No, the Jewish leaders just got madder.

John: Uh. Oh.

Megan: Filled with the Holy Spirit, Stephen looked up at heaven and saw the glory of God. Jesus was standing right there too.

Eric: Totally awesome!

Megan: Stephen said, "I see heaven open, and the Son of Man standing at the right hand of God."

Anna: I don't think he was helping himself by saying *that*.

John: I'm guessing the crowd went wild.

Megan: Ding, ding! We have two winners!

John: I'm starting to see why you think he was a hero.

Megan: The angry mob picked up stones, threw them at Stephen.

Eric: *(shocked, silent for a few seconds)* Was he killed?

Megan: Yes. Stephen was outnumbered. But he never backed down from telling people about Jesus. He stood his ground as long as he could. Then he called out to Jesus to take his soul.

Anna: *(shaking head)* I can't believe he died.

Megan: Before he died, Stephen asked God to forgive those who were hurting him.

John: I won't ever forget the story of Stephen. Where in the Bible can I read the whole story?

Megan: Start in chapter 6 of the book of Acts.

Eric: Superheroes come in human shapes and sizes. I didn't know that.

Anna: Now you know, little brother.

Stephen went face-to-face with a situation that is as bad as it gets. Stephen could have tried to run away to save his own life, but he didn't. He trusted God, and God was with Stephen. Most of us probably will never have to give our lives for our faith, although Christians in other parts of the world are put in prison and hurt for believing in Jesus. Wherever we live, God wants us to stand up and live for Christ. Who can stand and answer four questions about Stephen and our story?

Toss the four numbered balls to different parts of the room. Bring kids with the balls to the front one-by-one and ask these questions. Allow kids to get help from the group if they need it. After each correct answer, let kids drop the ball into a bag.

 ■ How would you describe today's Bible character Stephen in your own words?

 ■ Why was Stephen brought before the Jewish leaders?

 ■ Stephen asked God to do something for those stoning him. What was it?

 ■ What was the good news Stephen shared with others that cost him his life on earth?

The message that Stephen preached is not out of date. We need to hear the good news that Jesus loves us and forgives our sins. We need to know that God is with us, even in terrifying times.

Even when we can't see any way out of our trouble, God is there. For some, it's easy and natural to talk about Jesus. But for many of us, it's a hard thing to do. People might make fun of us or find ways to be mean. But we can learn from Stephen's story that God is with us throughout our lives, and he gives us the courage to tell other people about him. Jesus is on your side. In your shepherd groups you'll talk about courage to share the good news with other people.

Bible Verse
"Do not fear, for I am with you; do not be dismayed, for I am your God."
Isaiah 41:10

Dismiss kids to their shepherd groups.

② Shepherd's Spot

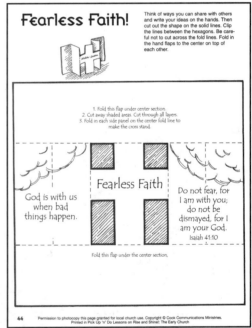

Gather your small group and help kids find Acts 6:8–15 and Acts 7:55—8:1 in their Bibles. Review the highlights of the Bible story or have volunteers take turns reading Acts 6:8–15, and Acts 7:55—8:1 aloud.

Stephen wasn't worried about what people thought about him or what might happen to him. He was so filled with the Spirit and the love of his Savior he simply had to let others know. God doesn't promise Christians a life without struggle. But he does promise to be with us in harsh times. In Jesus we find new life.

■ How do we know Stephen loved his enemies?
■ Where did Stephen get his power to do miracles and wonders and to stand up for Jesus?

Jesus died on the cross, then rose from the grave. Stephen knew God had power over death. You know that, too, don't you? **Let's cut and fold today's handout and make a fearless faith reminder.** Pass out the "Fearless Faith!" handout. Have kids follow the instructions on the handout.

Have a volunteer read Isaiah 41:10 from the handout: "Do not fear, for I am with you; do not be dismayed, for I am your God."

■ What keeps you from sharing Jesus with your friends?
■ Can you share God's love through your actions? How?

Share the good news! God will help us be brave. Invite kids to share concerns about sharing Jesus with their friends. **Then pray together. Dear Lord, please help us to be fearless in sharing you and your love with others. Please help us this week as we go to school or spend time with our friends. Help us live our lives in a way that brings people to you. In Jesus' name, amen.**

The "Fearless Faith!" handout:

Fearless Faith!

Think of ways you can share with others and write your ideas on the hands. Then cut out the shape on the solid lines. Clip the lines between the hexagons. Be careful not to cut across the fold lines. Fold in the hand flaps to the center on top of each other.

1. Fold this flap under center section.
2. Cut away shaded areas. Cut through all layers.
3. Fold in each side panel on the center fold line to make the cross stand.

God is with us when bad things happen.

Fearless Faith

Do not fear, for I am with you; do not be dismayed, for I am your God.
Isaiah 41:10

Fold this flap under the center section.

Fearless Faith!

1. Fold this flap under the center section.
2. Cut away shaded areas. Cut through all layers.
3. Fold in each side panel on the center fold line to make your cross stand.

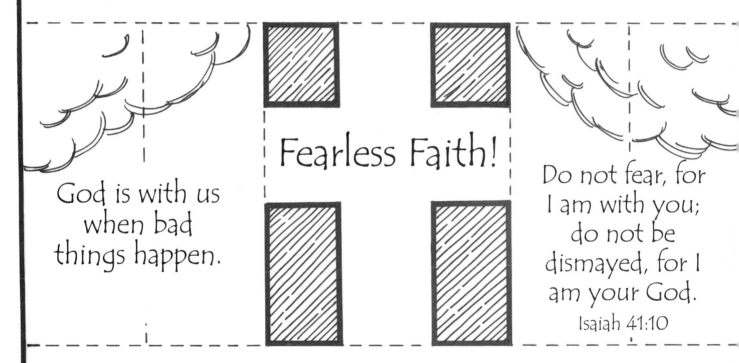

God is with us when bad things happen.

Fearless Faith!

Do not fear, for I am with you; do not be dismayed, for I am your God.

Isaiah 41:10

Fold this flap under the center section.

Workshop Wonders

Stephen had God-given courage and it helped him make a stand. And God upheld Stephen in a miraculous way.

■ **Do you remember how God helped Stephen? Share the story.**

Today's Bible story is amazing enough when we think how Stephen faced the angry crown with no one to help him. Hard, cold hearts persecuted him that day. Among those that stood and watched was a Roman named Saul. Saul held the coats, while others threw stones.

Saul stood by as others hurled rocks at Stephen. How would you feel about someone who didn't help you when you needed it? Would you be surprised to know that Saul would some-day become a Christian? At the time, Saul hated Christians. But later he became the apostle Paul. He loved Jesus with all his heart and he influenced the whole world for Christ. We will hear more about him in a later lesson.

God helps you take a stand for faith, even in tough times. You may never know the number of people watching you, wondering where you get the strength to stay strong. Pick someone to set up one domino. **Here is Stephen alone being strong for God. He influences two others.** Have someone place a domino on either side of the first one, equally spaced.

■ **When is it hard for you to let others know you believe in God?**
■ **What are some different ways you can tell others about God?**

Point to the two dominoes. **These two can influence two more.** Give the dominoes a tap and watch them fall. Now give your class the chance to help set up a long line of dominoes. Double dominos or form a more complicated design. **Take your time so we don't have any false starts! As you work, think on this: when we speak, sound vibrates forming a sound wave. One wave hits another and another and soon our words are heard. When we spread the word of God it touches a life which, in turn, touches another. Think of that when you line up your dominoes.**
You can be a hero! Put on courage and explain the love of Christ to someone who's never heard of him. Remember, we are called by Jesus to witness to others. Before time runs out, watch dominoes rows fall.

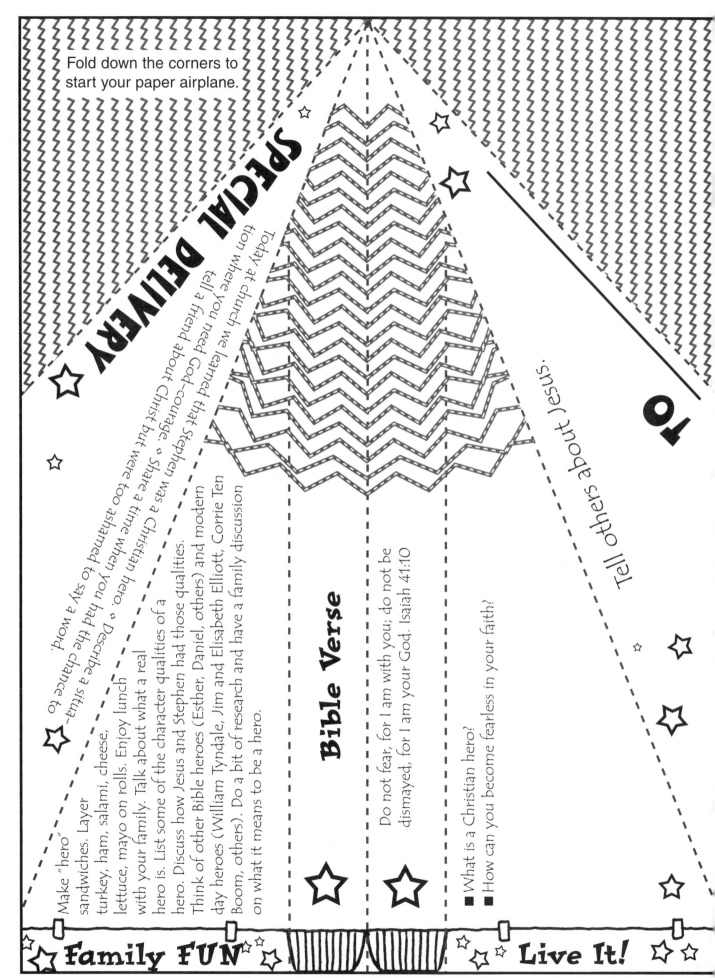

Fold down the corners to start your paper airplane.

SPECIAL DELIVERY

TO

Tell others about Jesus.

Today at church we learned that Stephen was a Christian hero. Describe a situation where you need God-courage. Share a time when you had the chance to tell a friend about Christ but were too ashamed to say a word.

Make "hero" sandwiches. Layer turkey, ham, salami, cheese, lettuce, mayo on rolls. Enjoy lunch with your family. Talk about what a real hero is. List some of the character qualities of a hero. Discuss how Jesus and Stephen had those qualities. Think of other Bible heroes (Esther, Daniel, others) and modern day heroes (William Tyndale, Jim and Elisabeth Elliott, Corrie Ten Boom, others). Do a bit of research and have a family discussion on what it means to be a hero.

Bible Verse

Do not fear, for I am with you; do not be dismayed, for I am your God. Isaiah 41:10

■ What is a Christian hero?
■ How can you become fearless in your faith?

Family FUN

Live It!

Tell Me More, Please!

Option

Get Set
LARGE GROUP ■ Greet kids and do a puppet skit. Schooner learns about being in the right place at the right time.
❏ large bird puppet ❏ puppeteer ❏ a picture of a chariot to show children

1

Bible 4U! Instant Drama
LARGE GROUP ■ An angel speaks and Philip listens. Hear all the adventure as Philip heads out and meets up with a Scripture-loving Ethiopian official.
❏ 6 actors ❏ two chairs ❏ Bible or paper scroll ❏ copies of pp. 50–51, "Wild Chariot Ride"script ❏ 4 numbered balls Optional: ❏ 2 Bibletime costumes, crepe paper chariot reins ❏ angel and horse costumes

2

Shepherd's Spot
SMALL GROUP ■ Use the "Good News Feet" handout to encourage kids to share the good news with others. Share concerns and pray together. Send home the Special Delivery handout.
❏ Bibles ❏ pencils ❏ scissors ❏ brads ❏ copies of p. 54, "Good News Feet"
❏ copies of p. 56, Special Delivery

Option

Workshop Wonders
SMALL GROUP ■ You decide! Have kids play a game that review the highlights of today's story or make simple handheld mazes.
❏ slips of paper ❏ pen ❏ hat or bowl
Optional: ❏ jar lids or oatmeal canister lids ❏ yarn ❏ glue ❏ hole punch
❏ 3" x 5" index cards ❏ markers ❏ beads or candy balls

Bible Basis
Philip and the Ethiopian official
Acts 8:4-6, 26-39

Learn It!
God works anywhere, anytime.

Live It!
Help others understand God's Word.

Bible Verse
As it is written, "'How beautiful are the feet of those who bring good news." Romans 10:15

8:4 Those who had been scattered preached the word wherever they went.
5 Philip went down to a city in Samaria and proclaimed the Christ there.
6 When the crowds heard Philip and saw the miraculous signs he did, they all paid close attention to what he said.
26 Now an angel of the Lord said to Philip, "Go south to the road—the desert road that goes down from Jerusalem to Gaza."
27 So he started out, and on his way he met an Ethiopian eunuch, an important official in charge of all the treasury of Candace, queen of the Ethiopians. This man had gone to Jerusalem to worship,
28 and on his way home was sitting in his chariot reading the book of Isaiah the prophet.
29 The Spirit told Philip, "Go to that chariot and stay near it."
30 Then Philip ran up to the chariot and heard the man reading Isaiah the prophet. "Do you understand what you are reading?" Philip asked.
31 "How can I," he said, "unless someone explains it to me?" So he invited Philip to come up and sit with him.
32 The eunuch was reading this passage of Scripture: "He was led like a sheep to the slaughter, and as a lamb before the shearer is silent, so he did not open his mouth.
33 In his humiliation he was deprived of justice. Who can speak of his descendants? For his life was taken from the earth."
34 The eunuch asked Philip, "Tell me, please, who is the prophet talking about, himself or someone else?"
35 Then Philip began with that very passage of Scripture and told him the good news about Jesus.
36 As they traveled along the road, they came to some water and the eunuch said, "Look, here is water. Why shouldn't I be baptized?"...
38 And he gave orders to stop the chariot. Then both Philip and the eunuch went down into the water and Philip baptized him.
39 When they came up out of the water, the Spirit of the Lord suddenly took Philip away, and the eunuch did not see him again, but went on his way rejoicing.

Insights

The number of Christians in Jerusalem grew to the point that they could not be treated as a passing fad, and believers came under persecution, even dying for the faith as Stephen did. Others were forced to scatter—but they took the gospel with them. Persecution that forced believers out of Jerusalem did not squelch the new faith, but rather multiplied it. Philip was one of the seven deacons selected to help care for the believers in Jerusalem, and now he became a popular evangelist, healing, preaching and casting out demons.

But sometimes the people God wants to reach are not in the crowds. An angel directed Philip to follow a chariot carrying an Ethiopian official. The man had been to Jerusalem to worship, so he was already attracted to the one true God. His thirst for understanding pulled him into God's Word. Here were no crowds, just one man puzzling over a passage of Scripture. However, he likely didn't have the benefit of traditional Jewish education, so the prophecies were a mystery. It wasn't unusual for people to read aloud even when they were alone. This gave Philip the perfect opportunity to offer to help the Ethiopian understand that the passage from Isaiah referred to Jesus Christ. The man's immediate response was belief and a desire to identify with Christ through baptism.

What would have happened if Philip had been so caught up in the crowds who followed him that he resisted the Spirit's nudging to go to a desert road? Or if he had not known the Scriptures as well as he did? Use this lesson to encourage kids to read and study God's Word so they can grow as Christians and share the good news.

Option Get Set

Hold up a picture of a chariot when you speak of it in today's puppet script. **Welcome. Before you sit, I want you to run in place while I count to 10. Ready? Go! 1-2-3-4-5-6-7-8-9-10. Great job! Now everyone have a good stretch, and sit.** *Schooner pops up.*

Schooner: Running is soooo inferior to flying, boss!

Leader: Hello, Schooner. It's wonderful you could join us.

Schooner: I always have time for my wingless two-legged friends!

Leader: Philip, the Bible character in today's story had a chance to help an important official understand the Word of God.

Schooner: And he rode a horse to meet him. Giddyup!

Leader: Actually he waited for an angel to finish speaking and then he ran.

Schooner: We had two angels in our very first story, remember boss? Anyway, riding would have been easier.

Leader: If you owned a horse.

Schooner: Or flying. I prefer to fly. *(spreads wings)*

Leader: You mention that, Schooner. Frequently.

Schooner: *(preens feathers)* Oh? Have I?

Leader: Philip couldn't fly.

Schooner: Too bad he wasn't a parrot.

Leader: Well, he wasn't a parrot, and he didn't ride a horse. He ran right up to a chariot, though. *(hold up a picture of a chariot)*

Schooner: A chariot? Sounds dangerous, if you ask me.

Leader: He was obeying God.

Schooner: Boss, God doesn't want people to get run over by chariots.

Leader: Philip didn't get run over.

Schooner: No?

Leader: No. God wanted him to talk to an important official in the chariot who had questions about what he was reading in the book of Isaiah. Isaiah was an Old Testament prophet.

Schooner: Why didn't the guy in the chariot just go to church? Everybody talks about God there.

Leader: In church, on the soccer field, at lunch, riding in a chariot. God wants us to bring the good news about his Son, Jesus wherever people happen to be.

Schooner: A man in a chariot? Can't quite picture that, boss.

Leader: Think of him sitting in a car then. Philip had a chance to explain God's Word to a man in a car. How's that?

Schooner: I get it, boss. Philip was in the right place at the right time. Start your engines! *Squawk!*

Leader: God works anywhere, anytime, Schooner. Because of Philip's skillful teaching the official believed in Jesus and was baptized.

Schooner: I'm not sure I could teach anyone God's Word.

Leader: Why not little bird?

Schooner: I'm not a pastor or a teacher. I've only been to Parrot Elementary School.

Leader: What did you learn?

Schooner: How to repeat words, squawk, eat crackers, bird tricks. The usual.

Leader: But you come here every week to help me teach.

Schooner: Oh yeah, there is that.

Leader: You know more about God's Word than you think you do, Schooner.

Schooner: You think so?

Leader: How long have we been together sharing the wisdom of God's Bible stories with children?

Schooner: *(whistles)* A long time. I have the gray feathers to prove it!

Leader: Schooner, you are surely a smartie pants bird.

Schooner: You said it, boss!

Leader: Calling all smart boys and girls— and parrot! Bible 4U! coming up.

Printed in Pick Up 'n' Do Lessons on Rise and Shine!: The Early Church

1 Bible 4U!

Being a Christian after Jesus returned to heaven was serious business. But every day more and more people became Christians. Soon they were not just a little group. The group was growing into the thousands.

As you might imagine, the Jewish religious leaders were not happy about this. That's when persecution began. Persecution means Christians were hurt and imprisoned for their belief in Jesus. It was a very hard time. To get away from the persecution, many Christians fled Jerusalem.

Instant Prep
Select six people to play the parts of Philip, an angel, a sick person, a horse, an Ethiopian official and a demon-possessed person. Give each a person copy of the "Wild Chariot Ride" script. Set out two chairs to be the chariot.

for Overachievers
Have a drama team prepare the story. Dress Philip and the two people he heals in Bibletime costumes. Dress the Ethiopian in bright colors, with a Bible or scroll. Give him crepe paper reins attached to the horse actor. The angel may have a white robe and white crepe paper streamers to suggest wings. Make ears and a tail for a horse costume. Prepare a backdrop that suggests the desert.

But even though believers ran away, they didn't stop talking about Jesus. Everywhere believers went, news about Jesus went too.

Philip was part of the crowd who left Jerusalem. In fact, he was one of the first Christian missionaries. One day God sent an angel to ask Philip to do something a little unusual. What could that be? Let's imagine we are all in Samaria, near the desert. Our story starts with Philip healing the sick.

Wild Chariot Ride
Based on Acts 8:4–6, 26–39

Philip is walking along and stops to speak to audience. Sick person sits on floor.

Philip: Hello. I'm Philip. I became a Christian in Jerusalem. Ever since then, I preach Jesus Christ risen from the dead and his saving grace. I left Jerusalem when the Romans began terrorizing Christians. Now I'm in Samaria, which is a little safer.

Sick person: Sir, in the name of God, please help me. I've heard you preach about a Savior. I'm sick and I can't walk. I believe that Jesus can heal me.

Philip: In the name of Jesus Christ and the power of the Holy Spirit, be healed. Get up and walk.

Sick person: *(gets up and dances)* I can walk! I can dance! I am healed! Praise God! Praise God! I must go and tell my friends! *(dances off stage)*

Actor runs in wildly.

Sick person: Help me! Please! There is evil inside me and it tries to throw me into the fire and harm me! I have tried everything to free myself. Please set me free from this demon.

Philip: In the name of Jesus Christ I command you, evil one, to leave this person and never return!

Sick person: Yes! I'm free, I'm free! Praise God! Praise Jesus Christ! *(dances off)*

Angel enters.

Angel: Psst! Philip. Over here.

Philip moves close to Angel.

Angel: You're a busy guy. You're hard to catch up with.

Philip: I have a job to spread the news: God can do anything, anywhere.

Angel: (*puts arm around Philip's shoulder*) You've been doing a great job with all the preaching in Samaria.

Philip. Thank you. God is the one who is doing the work.

Angel: Listen. Big change of plans. God told me to tell you to head south.

Philip: Why south?

Angel: You'll find a desert road. Take that road to the Gaza Desert.

Philip: The desert? Right now?

Angel: Yes, right now. Wait there and the Holy Spirit will tell you what to do next.

Angel leaves. Horse and Ethiopian enter.

Philip: Well, I'm in the desert, but I don't believe this. The Holy Spirit told me to go up to a chariot. I feel a little stupid doing this, but whatever God wants me to do I will do. God can work anywhere, anytime.

Philip runs in place or toward chariot.

Horse: (*neighs*) Do you believe it? This guy is chasing our chariot.

Philip: (*huffs, puffs*) The rider has fine clothes. He looks pretty important. He must be an official.

Ethiopian: (*loud and with emphasis*) "He was led like a sheep to the slaughter, and as a lamb before the shearer is silent, so he did not open his mouth."

Philip: (*huffs, puffs*) He's reading aloud. It sounds like a passage from Isaiah. I think I can catch up.

Ethiopian: (*sees Philip, pulls on reigns*) Whoa!

Horse: (*neighs*) Oh, well, I needed a rest anyway. Let's see what boy wonder wants with my boss.

Philip catches up with chariot.

Philip: (*huffs and takes a deep breath*) Hey! Thanks for stopping. I'm wondering what you're reading.

Ethiopian: I'm reading Isaiah, God's prophet. But I don't understand it.

Philip: Isaiah is one of my favorite writers!

Ethiopian: He's talking about a sheep or lamb to be killed. But I don't understand who he's talking about. Who is going to be killed like a lamb?

Philip: Great question!

Ethiopian: I hope you have a great answer.

Horse: (*neighs*) Look, bud! We've come a looooong way and I'm tired! Just tell my boss what he needs to know so I can get this chariot home.

Philip: Isaiah was talking about the Jewish Messiah, who died for our sins. If you agree, I can explain more about it.

Ethiopian: Please do. I came from Africa to Jerusalem to worship God there. The Jewish people have the one true God. But I have a feeling there's a lot more that I don't understand.

Horse: (*neighs*) Geez Louise. I have an itchy feeling this is going to take a while.

Philip and Ethiopian talk quietly, nodding and looking in Bible or scroll.

Philip: Now do you understand everything I have told you about Jesus?

Ethiopian: I still have a lot to learn. But I know that Jesus is the Messiah who died to forgive my sins. He rose from the dead and lives. I believe that Jesus is my Lord and Savior.

Philip: Welcome to the family, brother!

Ethiopian: (*pointing*) Look. There's water. Would you baptize me in the name of Jesus?

Philip: Sure, brother! Be happy to.

Horse: Oh, no! Now a baptism. No one at home will believe this story. I'm ready to gallop outta here—with or without the bossman.

Horse sneaks away and exits.

Bible 4U!

Jesus wants us to tell people about him. Sometimes, like the Ethiopian official in today's story, people come to us ready to discover more about Jesus and his power to forgive sin. Catch one of the balls and be ready to answer to a question on today's Bible story. Ready?

Toss the four numbered balls to different parts of the room. Bring kids with the balls to the front one-by-one and ask these questions. Allow kids to get help from the group if they need it. After each correct answer, let kids drop the ball into a bag.

 ■ Why did Philip travel to Samaria, then leave and go south to the desert?

 ■ The Ethiopian had gone to Jerusalem to worship the one true God. What did he need help with?

 ■ Who brought Philip and the Ethiopian together?

 ■ Why should we read and study the Bible? Is it okay to ask questions when we don't understand Scripture? Why or why not?

Philip and other Christians had to leave Jerusalem because Christians were being thrown into prison. The Roman and Jewish leaders did everything they could to stamp out Christianity. But once people knew that Jesus loved them and died for their sins, they wanted to share the good news with everyone. Christianity spread like wildfire. The Holy Spirit filled Christians and gave them power to do miracles in Jesus' name. So chasing Christians out of Jerusalem didn't put a stop to Christianity. In fact, it made it spread faster because now Christians were living all over the Roman Empire. God can work anywhere, anytime.

Philip was willing to do whatever God asked him to do, whether it was preaching or healing or casting out demons, or just talking to one person who had questions about God's Word. There's always time to study the Word of God. Often God empowers new meaning to words we've read many times. Today in your shepherd groups, you'll talk about what it means to study God's Word and help others understand it.

Bible Verse
As it is written, "How beautiful are the feet of those who bring good news." Romans 10:15

Dismiss kids to their shepherd groups.

② Shepherd's Spot

Gather your small group and help kids find Acts 8:4–6, 26–39 in their Bibles.

Philip lived in a time when Christians were being persecuted by the religious leaders and the Romans. Because of this they went to different parts of the world and the Christian faith grew even faster. The people who spread out from Jerusalem were ready to talk about Jesus. They knew that God could work anywhere, anytime.

Review the highlights of the Bible story or have volunteers take turns reading Acts 8:4–6, 26–39 aloud.

- **Do angels help people today? How did an angel help Philip?**
- **Philip was eager to help the Ethiopian official understand God's Word. Why?**
- **How does it help others trust us when we know answers to their questions about God and his Son, Jesus?**

Pass out the "Good News Feet" handout. Have kids follow the instructions on the handout to form a "walking world" paper craft.

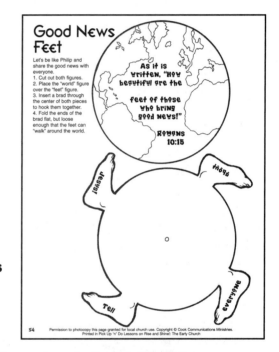

Read Romans 10:15 from the handout: "As it is written, 'How beautiful are the feet of those who bring good news!' "

- **What is the good news missionaries bring around the world?**
- **Family and friends can help us share Jesus. Go ahead and put feet on what you've learned! Name two things you and your family can do this weekend to make Jesus come alive to others.**

When you take your handout home, ask your parents to help you find a map. Find where Ethiopia is, in Africa. Find Jerusalem in Israel. Find the Gaza Desert. How far did Philip travel to reach the Ethiopian official? Remember, he probably walked all the way.

Let's all make time this year for praying and reading the Bible so we can be ready to help other people understand God's Word. Invite kids to share concerns about others who need to know God. Then pray. **Dear Lord, help us to share about you with others. Make our feet beautiful, as we walk through life and share the good news that God loves everyone. We pray for our friends and for people around the world who don't know you. In Jesus' name, amen.**

Good News Feet

Let's be like Philip and share the good news with everyone.

1. Cut out both figures.
2. Place the "world" figure over the "feet" figure.
3. Insert a brad through the center of both pieces to hook them together.
4. Fold the ends of the brad flat, but loose enough that the feet can "walk" around the world.

As it is written, "How beautiful are the

feet of those who bring good news!"

Romans 10:15

everyone

about

Tell

Jesus!

Workshop Wonders

Before class, write the following categories on slips of paper: Philip; the angel's instructions; the Ethiopian official; what Philip told the Ethiopian; parts of the good news; places where God can work. Fold up the slips and put them in a hat or bowl

In today's story we learned that God stirs hearts to work for him anywhere, anytime. There was Philip in Samaria, proclaiming Christ, ready and willing to do what God asked him to do. God knew the Ethiopian man had a spiritual hunger and that he would need to know the answers to his questions. So God helped Philip to be right there, in the nick of time, with the answer. Because Philip listened to God he had an opportunity to teach someone who really needed to know. He was able to answer the Ethiopian's questions and help the man believe in Jesus.

Get List:
- ☐ slips of paper
- ☐ pen
- ☐ hat or bowl
  Optional:
- ☐ jar lids or oatmeal canister lids
- ☐ yarn
- ☐ glue
- ☐ hole punch
- ☐ index cards
- ☐ markers
- ☐ beads or candy balls

- ■ **Have you ever had the chance to explain a Bible story to someone else? What happened?**
- ■ **What if you don't know all the answers to teach someone else? Where can you get help?**

Let's get some practice helping others learn about God by playing the "Be the Teacher!" Bible game. Assign the kids to groups of three or four. Pick one child from each group to begin as "teacher." Have the "teacher" of the first group draw a category and "teach" that category to his or her group. The teacher can give hints by saying simple sentences or listing items that fit the category, but the teacher cannot use any words on the slip of paper. Give a maximum time limit of one minute. (Adjust time as appropriate to your group.) After the group has guessed or time is up, confirm the answer and go on to the next group. Play until everyone who wants to be the "teacher" has a turn. Repeat categories or make up some more.

- ■ **On a scale of 1–10 how frustrating was it when you couldn't get the answer across to your team?**
- ■ **How did you feel when a classmate figured out what you were teaching?**

Option: Today's Bible verse states, "How beautiful are the feet of those who bring good news!" Make simple handheld mazes that remind children of the "travel" and "paths" happy feet take. Before class, gather enough jar lids or oatmeal canister lids for your group. Make hand mazes in two ways—by gluing yarn in a circular pattern inside the lid (see illustration) or by hole punching a double layer of index cards and then cutting the cards to fit snugly inside the lids. (If you choose, punch holes in a pattern to represent a "stepping stone" path.) Drop beads or candy balls inside the maze and watch them travel between yarn paths or in and out of the "stepping stones." Kids can personalize their mazes with markers before they glue.

You might not think feet are beautiful, but God can use each pair to teach others his holy Word!

Fold down the corners to start your paper airplane.

SPECIAL DELIVERY

TO

★ Help others understand God's Word.

Today at church we learned that an angel sent Philip to find a chariot in the desert and tell the good news." What's your favorite thing to say to others about Jesus? What do you think it would be like if an angel talked to you? What is your favorite Bible verse?

Draw a picture of the world on a large piece of paper. Then draw outlines of "walking feet" on the world. Fill feet in with Bible verses. Spend time this week praying for countries you find on a map or study in school. Pray for missionaries in those countries. Pray for their safety, their Christian walk, their families, for wisdom, and that God would meet all their needs. Remember, God works anywhere, anytime.

Bible Verse

As it is written, "How beautiful are the feet of those who bring good news!" Romans 10:15

■ What supplies will you need to tell others of the risen Savior? How much will you have to prepare?
■ Think of someone today who needs to hear the good news. When can you share it?

Family FUN

Live It!

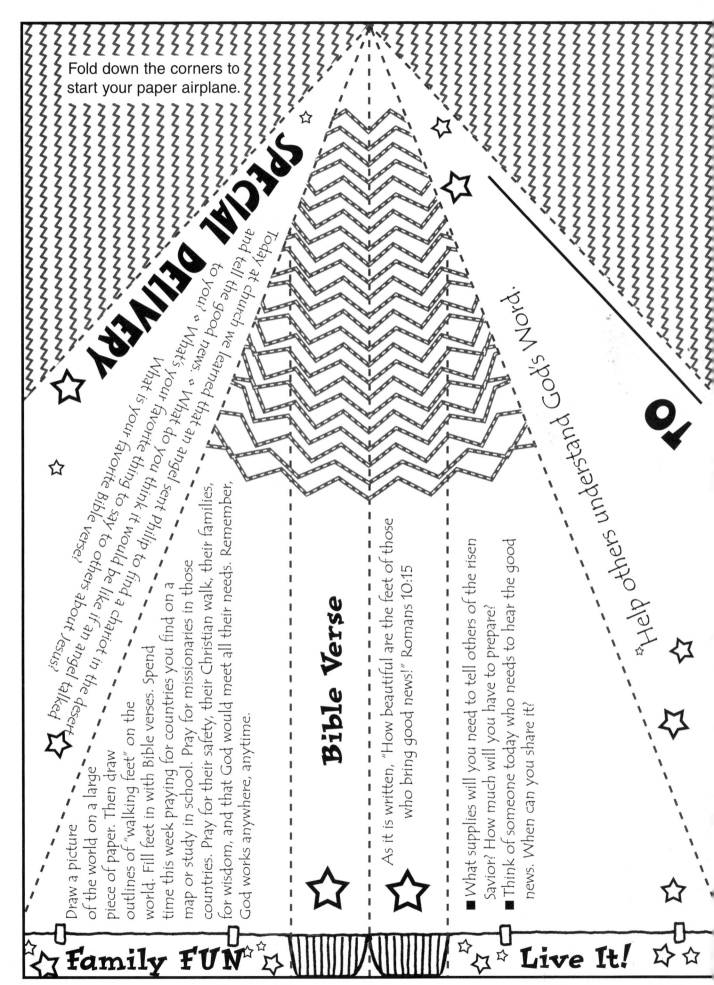

Saul's Heart of Stone

Option — Get Set
LARGE GROUP ■ Greet kids and do a puppet skit. Schooner sees what he remembers about a Bible character named Saul.
❑ large bird puppet   ❑ puppeteer

1 — Bible 4U! Instant Drama
LARGE GROUP ■ Actors present a dramatic account of how Saul met Jesus on the road to the city of Damascus.
❑ 5 actors   ❑ copies of pp. 60–61, "Blind, But Now I See" script
❑ 4 numbered balls   Optional: ❑ Bibletime costumes   ❑ maps   ❑ sunglasses
❑ stack of papers

2 — Shepherd's Spot
SMALL GROUP ■ Use the "Change of Heart" handout to encourage kids to think about friends who need an invitation to know Jesus. Share concerns and pray together. Send home the Special Delivery handout.
❑ Bibles   ❑ pencils   ❑ scissors   ❑ copies of p. 64, "Change of Heart"
❑ copies of p. 66, Special Delivery

Option — Workshop Wonders
SMALL GROUP ■ Fun science! A science demonstration with aluminum foil and combs helps kids think about attracting people to Jesus.
❑ combs and scissors (enough for your group)   ❑ aluminum foil

Bible Basis
Saul's conversion.
Acts 9:1–19

Learn It!
God can change even the hardest heart.

Live It!
Invite everyone to know Jesus.

Bible Verse
If anyone is in Christ, he is a new creation; the old is gone, the new has come.
2 Corinthians 5:17

Quick Takes

9:1 Meanwhile, Saul was still breathing out murderous threats against the Lord's disciples. He went to the high priest
2 and asked him for letters to the synagogues in Damascus, so that if he found any there who belonged to the Way, whether men or women, he might take them as prisoners to Jerusalem.
3 As he neared Damascus on his journey, suddenly a light from heaven flashed around him.
4 He fell to the ground and heard a voice say to him, "Saul, Saul, why do you persecute me?"
5 "Who are you, Lord?" Saul asked. "I am Jesus, whom you are persecuting," he replied.
6 "Now get up and go into the city, and you will be told what you must do."
7 The men traveling with Saul stood there speechless; they heard the sound but did not see anyone.
8 Saul got up from the ground, but when he opened his eyes he could see nothing. So they led him by the hand into Damascus.
9 For three days he was blind, and did not eat or drink anything.
10 In Damascus there was a disciple named Ananias. The Lord called to him in a vision, "Ananias!" "Yes, Lord," he answered.
11 The Lord told him, "Go to the house of Judas on Straight Street and ask for a man from Tarsus named Saul, for he is praying.
12 "In a vision he has seen a man named Ananias come and place his hands on him to restore his sight."
13 "Lord," Ananias answered, "I have heard many reports about this man and all the harm he has done to your saints in Jerusalem.
14 "And he has come here with authority from the chief priests to arrest all who call on your name."
15 But the Lord said to Ananias, "Go! This man is my chosen instrument to carry my name before the Gentiles and their kings and before the people of Israel.
16 "I will show him how much he must suffer for my name."
17 Then Ananias went to the house and entered it. Placing his hands on Saul, he said, "Brother Saul, the Lord—Jesus, who appeared to you on the road as you were coming here—has sent me so that you may see again and be filled with the Holy Spirit."
18 Immediately, something like scales fell from Saul's eyes, and he could see again. He got up and was baptized,
19 and after taking some food, he regained his strength. Saul spent several days with the disciples in Damascus.

Paul of Tarsus (in modern-day Turkey) was a Roman citizen. He lived from AD 3 or 5 to AD 67. Paul was a Jewish Pharisee, an elitist who studied and strictly followed Jewish law. He was highly educated and understood Greek. Paul was a zealot, meaning he was an extremely strong believer in following Jewish law. This was why he hunted down and persecuted Jewish Christians. He held the coats of those who stoned Stephen and witnessed Stephen's strong testimony.

Damascus was about 150 miles from Jerusalem, a distance that would probably take five or six days to travel. Although it was in the Roman province of Syria, it had a large Jewish population, and apparently enough of them were becoming Christians to warrant Paul's attention. Paul left Jerusalem with the legal authority to take prisoners, but he arrived in Damascus blind and bewildered. Somewhere on that road, Jesus blinded Paul with his presence. As an educated

Insights

Jew, Paul knew that the flash and voice from heaven meant the presence of God. Most likely no one would ever have argued Paul into the kingdom of God, but God wanted him for the kingdom and drew him in by an indisputable experience.

At first Christians were not sure what to make of this. Ananias resisted when God told him to go meet Saul. When he returned to Jerusalem, the disciples were afraid of him. Yet Paul went on to become the great apostle, who evangelized across the expanse of the Roman Empire. During those journeys, Paul was mistreated, beaten, imprisoned, but his faith held firm. It is generally believed soldiers of the Roman emperor Nero beheaded him for his faith.

We all know people who don't believe in God or Jesus Christ. Some are our loved ones. Use this lesson to show children that God can change even the hardest hearts.

Get Set

Read Acts 9:1 aloud. **"Saul was still breathing out murderous threats against the Lord's disciples."** Raise your hand if you remember the Bible character Saul from our Bible story two weeks ago. (Pause.) Saul was a minor character but he allowed a terrible thing to happen to a Christian leader named Steven. Let's ask Schooner. Schooner, come up here. *Schooner pops up.*

Schooner: Yep, boss? Here I am.

Leader: Got memory?

Schooner: I've got a memory like an elephant, and I even like peanuts, boss.

Leader: Okay, Schooner, do you remember a Bible character named Saul?

Schooner: Saul? Of course...Saul? Let's see, um, didn't he...wasn't he...?

Leader: Do you need some peanuts to jog your memory?

Schooner: No, no. I'll get it. Saul...um...he... Okay, I give up. *Squawk!*

Leader: Two weeks ago we heard a sad story about a Christian of the early church named Stephen. An angry crowd threw rocks at him.

Schooner: Yes, yes, yes. And Stephen asked God to forgive the crowd.

Leader: That's right. In that story Saul was holding the coats for the people throwing the stones.

Schooner: Ooohhh, yeeaahhh. I remember. He was a bad guy. Definitely a bad guy.

Leader: Today's story tells how Saul put in prison anyone he found who believed Jesus.

Schooner: Jail is like a cage, isn't it?

Leader: Yes, like a cage.

Schooner: I don't like cages, boss.

Leader: I understand my little bird friend.

Schooner: And I certainly don't like mean people.

Leader: The early Christians hated Saul. He separated families and didn't care who he hurt or put in prison.

Schooner: *(ruffles feathers and appears upset)* Squawk!

Leader: Yet, God looked deep inside Saul and saw a man he could use to spread the Christian faith.

Schooner: Wait a minute, boss. Mean ole Saul? I think you have your Bible guys mixed up.

Leader: No. God had a purpose for Saul.

Schooner: Changing a bad guy to a good guy is impossible, boss.

Leader: God will change Saul from the inside out.

Schooner: *(shakes head)* Nope. Saul is a bad guy. He's hopeless.

Leader: No one is hopeless in the eyes of God. God can change stone hearts to hearts that are soft and lovable and faithful.

Schooner: Hey, wait a minute. Are you trying to tell me that God changed terrible Saul to a kind and Jesus–lovin' man?

Leader: Well, yes, I am.

Schooner: *(shakes head)* Don't believe it.

Leader: God didn't give up on Saul even when Saul was hurting Christians.

Schooner: What did God do to get his attention?

Leader: Crash! Boom! Bang! It was pretty spectacular.

Schooner: Bring on the story, boss. This sounds too incredible to be true.

Leader: Bible 4U! will tell us all the amazing details.

① Bible 4U!

Welcome to today's edition of Bible 4U! Theater. A person who shows no grace or mercy to others and has no plans to change has a hard heart. Picture a heart inside a shell. Good feelings can't touch it. And it is very hard to break open.

Saul was an educated and powerful Pharisee and he hated Christians. He encouraged an angry mob to stone Stephen to death. He traveled all over the country hunting for Christians to take them back to Jerusalem to face a life of prison and hardship.

But God can change even the hardest heart, and he changed Saul's heart—in the blink of an eye.

Today's story tells us how God blinded Saul to get his attention. That's right, blinded him. Let's listen and find out how God changed hard hearted Saul while on the way to bully those that loved the Lord Jesus Christ.

Blind, But Now I See

Based on Acts 9:1–19

Saul and his Companion enter. They carry backpacks, maps and a big stack of papers.

Saul: *(looking fierce, fidgeting while looking at a map)* I have been waiting long enough for this trip to Damascus. Let's hit the road!

Companion: Are you sure you have everything? You don't have much luggage.

Saul: I don't need it. I'm on the hunt for Christians, and I want plenty of free hands to drag them back to Jerusalem.

Companion: Aren't there enough Christians to bully right here?

Saul: Christians are like rats. They keep multiplying. As soon as I close down one church here, two more spring up somewhere else.

Companion: Who do you plan to arrest in Damascus?

Saul: Men. Women. Children. I'll take them prisoner and bring them back to Jerusalem to face the religious court. It won't be pretty.

Companion: Do you have the arrest papers that the high priest gave you?

Saul: *(shows large stack of papers)* Right here. I'm all set to bring back as many Christians as I can get my hands on. Know this. The Jewish law is how I live my life. There is no other authority than that. Enough talk. Let's move.

Narrator: Saul and his companions set out on their journey. It would take several days for them to go from Jerusalem to Damascus. But as they traveled on the road, suddenly…

Special effects crew flashes the lights. Saul falls to the floor, throwing the arrest papers in the air. Companion remains standing. The voice of Jesus comes from off stage.

Jesus: Saul! Saul! Why do you persecute me?

Saul: *(with his face to the floor)* Who are you, Lord?

Jesus: You know who I am. I'm Jesus the Christ, the one you are causing so much trouble for. Get up and go to Damascus. Someone there will tell you what to do. Go!

Saul: *(getting up, feeling around as if blind)* I...I can't see.

Companion: *(grabs hold of Saul)* I heard something, but I didn't understand any of it. What happened?

Saul: We have to go to Damascus.

Companion: That's where we were planning to go.

Saul: Forget the arrest papers. I have to go and wait for someone.

Companion: Wait for who?

Saul: I'm not sure.

Companion: That doesn't sound like you, Saul. You're sure about everything.

Saul: We have to go to Damascus and wait. Let's go.

Companion: Something's changed here. I can feel it.

Saul: *(stumbles)* Help me. I can't see a thing. *(Saul slips on sunglasses.)*

Companion takes Saul by the arm and leads him across the stage to home interior set. Saul sits. Companion exits.

Narrator: Meanwhile, in Damascus God had a surprise for a Christian named Ananias. In a vision, Ananias heard from God.

Ananias enters opposite home set.

Jesus: Ananias!

Ananias: Lord, is that you?

Jesus: I have a job for you.

Ananias: Lord, anything.

Jesus: Go to Straight Street. Find the house of Judas. Ask for a man named Saul.

Ananias: *(terrified)* Saul of Tarsus! You mean the persecutor Saul? He's in town? He's a murderer. I don't want to go anywhere near him.

Jesus: I want you to go.

Ananias: But...but I've heard what he does to Christians in Jerusalem. If he's in Damascus now, he must have the authority of the high priest to arrest us on sight. I hate to argue with you, Lord, but this is not a good idea.

Jesus: I have big plans for Saul. He's will spread the Word of God and preach about me to the corners of the earth.

Ananias: *(still nervous but shrugs)* What can I do but obey my God? I'll go.

Ananias crosses stage to where Saul is sitting.

Narrator: By this time, Saul had lived in blindness for three days. And he hadn't had anything to eat or drink during that time either.

Ananias: I'm looking for Saul.

Saul: You found him. That's me. Are you Ananias?

Ananias: *(surprised)* Yes, I am.

Saul: I've been waiting for you. God told me in a vision you would come.

Ananias: I don't understand, but I'm here because God told me to come.

Saul: And I'm here because he told me to come to Damascus and wait for you. I'm blind but I saw Jesus!

Ananias: You blindness will be lifted. *(puts a hand on Saul's shoulder)* Brother Saul, the Lord Jesus who appeared to you on the road has sent me. He wants you to see again and be filled with the Holy Spirit.

Saul: *(opens eyes or takes off sunglasses)* I can see! I can see! Please, I want to be baptized.

Ananias: Right away. After that, you should have something to eat. You need get your strength back. God has amazing plans for you brother.

All exit.

In a flash, Saul met Jesus on the road to Damascus and suddenly he was a changed man. The old is gone, the new has come. God's power is greater than evil. And it pries hard hearts apart. God's power made Saul a new man. Saul would soon be known as Paul and would go on to become one of the greatest missionaries of all time. Let's see if you can catch four questions about Saul.

Toss the four numbered balls to different parts of the room. Bring kids with the balls to the front one-by-one and ask these questions. Allow kids to get help from the group if they need it. After each correct answer, let kids drop the ball into a bag.

 ■ **Why were Christians terrified of Saul from Tarsus?**

 ■ **Why was Saul going to the city of Damascus?**

 ■ **Why was Ananias afraid to obey God?**

 ■ **In what dramatic fashion did God change Saul? How could someone who hated Christians like no other become one of them?**

God worked in the hearts of both Ananias and Saul. Ananias was fearful of arrest by Saul. Yet he obeyed God. Ananias trusted that God had a plan, even if he didn't understand it. Think how surprised and relieved Ananias must have been when he met Saul and heard his story.

Saul stepped into God's kingdom that day. Saul became Paul. Instead of trying to hurt Christians, he wanted more Christians. Amazing! Paul wanted people to know Jesus the way the early church believers did— in love and grace and servanthood. Paul learned to love and trust Jesus with his life. Did you know, Paul wrote parts of the New Testament in the Bible? Today in your shepherd groups, you'll talk about how God changes hearts.

Bible Verse
If anyone is in Christ, he is a new creation; the old is gone, the new has come.
2 Corinthians 5:17

Dismiss kids to their shepherd groups.

2 Shepherd's Spot

Gather your small group and help kids find Acts 9:1–19 in their Bibles. Review the highlights of the story together.

Saul was a Roman citizen, a Jewish Pharisee. He studied and strictly followed Jewish law. This was why he hunted down and persecuted Jewish Christians with a vengeance—and held the coats of those who stoned Stephen. Saul wanted the Christian faith gone forever. On that day he witnessed Stephen's strong testimony. Did it change his heart? It did not. Only Jesus presence within a miraculous flash of light could do that.

Saul was blinded in his heart just as strongly as he was blinded in his eyes. He couldn't see the truth until Jesus showed it to him. Many of us are like Saul.

■ God can change even the hardest heart. Do you ever read or hear about hurtful and cruel people in the news? Are they hard-hearted like Saul? Should we pray for them? Remember, Saul changed and became a great missionary for Christ.

Pass out the "Change of Heart" handout. Help kids follow the instructions on the handout.

Have a volunteer read 2 Corinthians 5:17 from the handout: If anyone is in Christ, he is a new creation; the old is gone, the new has come.

Our handout today is a reminder to invite other people to know Jesus and let him change their hearts. When you take your handout home, ask your parents to help you remember to pray for people who don't know Jesus.

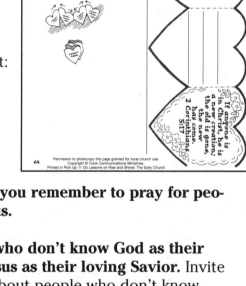

Change of Heart

1. Cut off the heart strip. Cut out the hearts in the strip on the solid lines, or fold the hearts over each other and cut them all together.
2. Open the heart strip and lay it flat. On the blank lines on the third heart, write names of people you can invite to know Jesus.
3. Fold the hearts in half on the center fold line, with the writing to the inside.
4. Fold back the outside hearts to form the front and back of the stack of hearts.

God can change even the hardest heart.

Invite everyone to know Jesus.

If anyone is in Christ, he is a new creation; the old is gone, the new has come. 2 Corinthians 5:17

Let's pray for people who don't know God as their heavenly Father and Jesus as their loving Savior. Invite kids to share concerns about people who don't know Jesus. **Dear Lord, we love you. Thank you for loving us enough to come to earth and die for our sins. We pray for people who don't know you and ask you to help us find ways to invite them to know you. We especially pray for** (pause for kids to mention names). **We pray in the name of Jesus Christ, amen.**

63

Change of Heart

1. Cut off the heart strip. Cut out the hearts in the strip on the solid lines, or fold the hearts over each other and cut them all together.
2. Open the heart strip and lay it flat. On the blank lines on the third heart, write names of people you can invite to know Jesus.
3. Fold the hearts in half on the center fold line, with the writing to the inside.
4. Fold back the outside hearts to form the front and back of the stack of hearts.

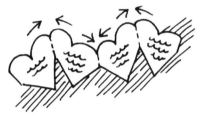

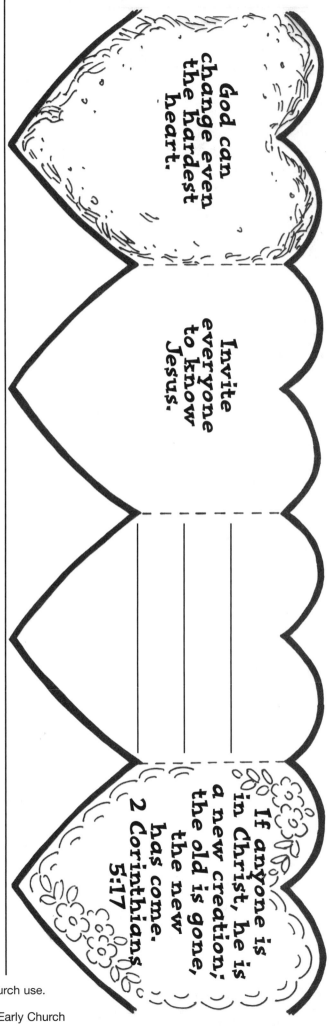

God can change even the hardest heart.

Invite everyone to know Jesus.

If anyone is in Christ, he is a new creation; the old is gone, the new has come. 2 Corinthians 5:17

Workshop Wonders

Set out foil, scissors and combs. **Our story began with Saul determined to destroy the Christian faith wherever he found it. Saul seemed unmovable, with a heart as hard as rock. Then he met Jesus and in a blaze of light got his attention! Saul became a believer. People who knew Saul before weren't sure they believed his change of heart. But he had changed. God can change the hardest heart, and he changed Saul's. Saul changed his name to Paul and became a great missionary. He traveled all over inviting everyone to know Jesus.**

Get List:
- ☐ aluminum foil
- ☐ scissors
- ☐ combs

- ■ If you had known Saul before he met Jesus on that road, would you have thought he could change? Why or why not?
- ■ How does this story give you hope for those who say they do not believe in Jesus?

Ask kids to find 2 Corinthians 5:17 in their Bibles and read it together: "If anyone is in Christ, he is a new creation; the old is gone, the new is come."

Jesus performed a miracle and Saul's heart changed. As different as night is to day, the old Saul was gone, and the new Paul burned bright. Surely not everyone will meet Jesus in a blaze of light in the middle of the road like Saul. Instead, we shine the light of Jesus by the way we live. When we do, we attract people. They notice our splendid behavior. We're truthful, helpful, kind and slow to anger. All very good things! Let's perform a fun science experiment that reminds us to attract people to Jesus.

Have kids cut 10 tiny pieces of aluminum foil and lay them on the table in front of them. Distribute combs. Instruct your group to move the combs quickly through their hair 10 times or more. (Hair must be clean and dry for this experiment to work.) Finally, hold the comb slightly above the foil pieces and watch what happens. The foil pieces "jump" toward the comb.

Allow kids to repeat the experiment a number of times. Notice that different bits of foil jump with each try. *Ask kids if they can explain why this happens.* Fun science fact: In the experiment, the comb becomes negatively charged as it travels through hair, picking up electrons as it goes. Aluminum foil has both negative and positive electrons. When the negatively charged comb is placed near the foil, the negative electrons in the foil "repel" or move away, leaving the positive electrons on the surface of the metal. These positive electrons are attracted to the negative electrons in the comb and thus "dance" toward the comb.

- ■ What attracts you to your friends? What qualities in you do others notice? How does this help bring others to Jesus?

Try this simple experiment at home with your families and talk about the many ways your family can attract others to the wonder, love and power of Jesus.

Fold down the corners to start your paper airplane.

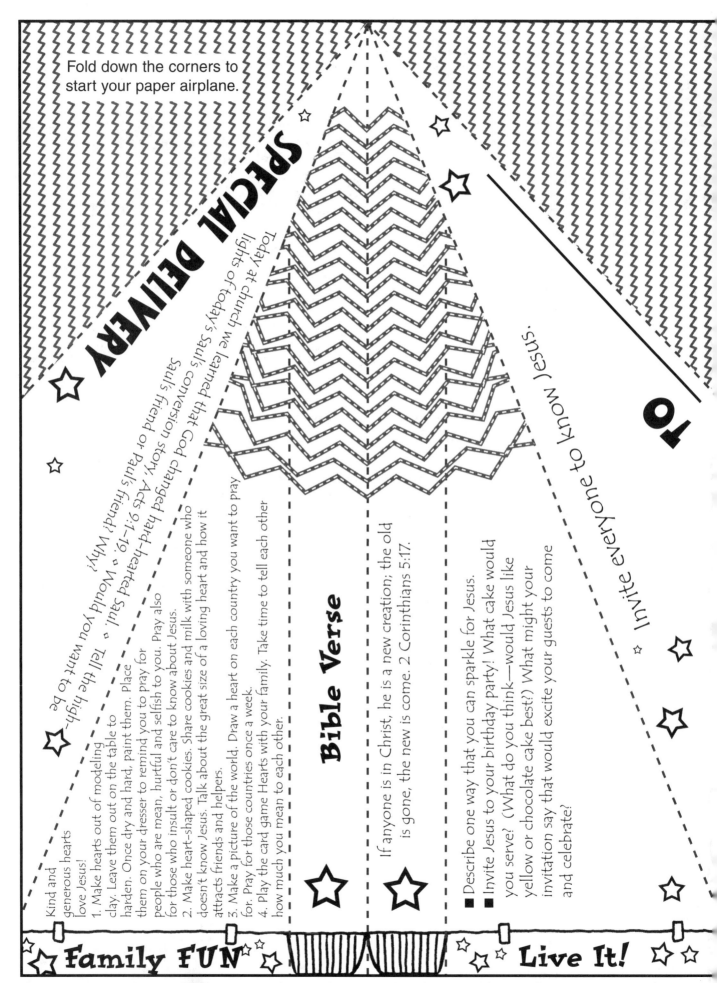

SPECIAL DELIVERY

TO

Invite everyone to know Jesus.

Today at church we learned that God changed hard-hearted Saul's heart. Saul's conversion story: Acts 9:1–19. Saul's friend or Paul's friend? Tell the high-lights of today's story. Would you want to be Saul's friend or Paul's friend? Why?

Kind and generous hearts love Jesus!

1. Make hearts out of modeling clay. Leave them out on the table to harden. Once dry and hard, paint them. Place them on your dresser to remind you to pray for people who are mean, hurtful and selfish to you. Pray also for those who insult or don't care to know about Jesus.

2. Make heart-shaped cookies. Share cookies and milk with someone who doesn't know Jesus. Talk about the great size of a loving heart and how it attracts friends and helpers.

3. Make a picture of the world. Draw a heart on each country you want to pray for. Pray for those countries once a week.

4. Play the card game Hearts with your family. Take time to tell each other how much you mean to each other.

Bible Verse

If anyone is in Christ, he is a new creation; the old is gone, the new is come. 2 Corinthians 5:17.

■ Describe one way that you can sparkle for Jesus.
■ Invite Jesus to your birthday party! What cake would you serve? (What do you think—would Jesus like yellow or chocolate cake best?) What might your invitation say that would excite your guests to come and celebrate?

Family FUN

Live It!

A Real Life Miracle for Tabitha

Option

Get Set
LARGE GROUP ■ Greet kids and do a puppet skit. Schooner discovers light! And that God's power helps people believe in him.
❑ large bird puppet ❑ puppeteer ❑ pan lids ❑ flashlight

1

Bible 4U! Instant Drama
LARGE GROUP ■ In today's drama, a young widow writes a letter to her friend describing the miraculous events at Joppa.
❑ 4 girl actors ❑ copies of pp. 70-71, "Tabitha, Wake Up!" script
❑ 4 numbered balls Optional: ❑ Bibletime costumes and backdrop
❑ fabric and sewing supplies

2

Shepherd's Spot
SMALL GROUP ■ Use the "Power Pack" handout to encourage kids to have faith in God's power. Share concerns and pray together. Send home the Special Delivery handout.
❑ Bibles ❑ pencils ❑ scissors ❑ copies of p. 74, "Power Pack"
❑ copies of p. 76, Special Delivery

Option

Workshop Wonder *
■ You choose! Play a flashlight hide-and-seek game or choose to watch smiles light up. Talk about shining the light of God's power.
❑ flashlight with removable batteries.
Optional: ❑ Wintergreen Lifesaver® candies ❑ hand mirrors

*Check with parents for any food allergies children may have.

Bible Basis
Peter prays and Tabitha lives again.
Acts 9:36–42

Learn It!
God's power helps us believe in him.

Live It!
Pray for God to show his power.

Bible Verse
You are the God who performs miracles; you display your power among the peoples.
Psalm 77:14

Quick Takes

Acts 9:36–42

36 In Joppa there was a disciple named Tabitha (which, when translated, is Dorcas), who was always doing good and helping the poor.
37 About that time she became sick and died, and her body was washed and placed in an upstairs room.
38 Lydda was near Joppa; so when the disciples heard that Peter was in Lydda, they sent two men to him and urged him, "Please come at once!"
39 Peter went with them, and when he arrived he was taken upstairs to the room. All the widows stood around him, crying and showing him the robes and other clothing that Dorcas had made while she was still with them.
40 Peter sent them all out of the room; then he got down on his knees and prayed. Turning toward the dead woman, he said, "Tabitha, get up." She opened her eyes, and seeing Peter she sat up.
41 He took her by the hand and helped her to her feet. Then he called the believers and the widows and presented her to them alive.
42 This became known all over Joppa, and many people believed in the Lord.

Insights

The town of Joppa (now Jaffa, a suburb of Tel Aviv) is one of the oldest cities in Israel. It was an important port on the Mediterranean seacoast and significant in the nation's history. The cedars of Lebanon used for the temple were floated into Joppa before being shipped to Jerusalem. Jonah left from Joppa when he ran from the Lord's instructions. After Herod the Great was named king of Judea, he began building up Caesarea, to the north, and the economic role of Joppa declined.

Joppa had its share of the poor, perhaps exacerbated by being eclipsed by Caesarea. It's clear from the outpouring after her death that Tabitha dedicated her life to helping the poor, particularly widows. She used her skill with a needle to meet practical needs.

When Tabitha died unexpectedly, people were so upset they send for Simon Peter, who was about 12 miles away in Lydda. Peter prayed for what was humanly impossible—the return of Tabitha to life. But Peter had been with Jesus on several occasions when Jesus raised the dead (Jairus's daughter, the widow's son in Nain, and Lazarus). Peter prayed for Tabitha with faith in the same power that returned these others from the dead.

This miraculous demonstration of the power of God gave everyone hope and joy. Nothing is impossible for God. Use this lesson to encourage kids to be encouraged to pray for God to use his power today.

Option Get Set

Before class remove the batteries from a flashlight. Keep both the flashlight and batteries handy. Collect pan lids that will make a crashing sound when dropped. **Welcome everyone. Good news! Find a place to sit, and get ready to hear a miracle story. We serve an amazing God who can do astonishing things.** *Crashing noise is heard.* **Schooner, is that you?** *More crashing sounds. Schooner pops up.*

Schooner: Yeah, boss.

Leader: What are you doing?

Schooner: I was looking for my roller skates.

Leader: Roller skates? You can't roller skate!

Schooner: You never know, boss, until you try.

Leader: *(scratch head)* You're a wonder, Schooner.

Schooner: *(annoyed)* I haven't found the skates yet.

Leader: Have you looked anywhere else?

Schooner: I'm sure they're in the closest. I just have to keep winging around. *(pops down)*

Leader: You mean feeling around.

Schooner: You feel, I wing, boss. It's dark in there.

Leader: Why don't you turn the light on?

Schooner: The closet doesn't have a light.

Leader: What about a flashlight? That would give you the light you need.

Schooner: *(pops up)*Oh, I don't believe in flashlights.

Leader: What? How can you not believe in flashlights?

Schooner: They don't work.

Leader: What do you mean they don't work?

Schooner: I tried using one, but it didn't work.

Leader: This one? *(picks up flashlight)*

Schooner: Yeah, that's the one. I pushed the button. And it didn't go on. *(shaking head)* Then I shook it.

Leader: Let me guess, it still didn't work.

Schooner: I even yelled at it. Nothing.

Leader: Hmm. Now you think flashlights never work.

Schooner: It's as obvious as the beak on my face.

Leader: *(leader looks at flashlight)* Well, no wonder, Schooner. There's no power. There are no batteries in this flashlight. *(puts the batteries in)*

Schooner: Batteries?

Leader: Watch. *(turns on flashlight)* With power it works. Do you believe in them now?

Schooner: I guess I do. Seeing is believing.

Leader: In today's story, God loves a faithful and kind woman, named Tabitha.

Schooner: What kindness did Tabitha show?

Leader: She made clothes.

Schooner: With needle and thread?

Leader: She sewed for her friends and the poor people of Joppa. Neighbors and friends loved Tabitha. She was generous to others. Tabitha was a kind disciple and believer of Jesus.

Schooner: So…Tabitha just gave the clothes away? Free of charge?

Leader: That's right.

Schooner: *Squawk!* That was a lovely idea, boss. Clothes to brighten the day. If feels good to have something new to wear!

Leader: The story doesn't end there, Schooner. The light gets brighter.

Schooner: How?

Leader: Today's story is a miracle story so hold on to your hat. One day Tabitha became ill and died.

Schooner: No!

Leader: But what should be a sad, sad story is not a sad story at all.

Schooner: *(dances a parrot jig)* I feel a miracle coming on!

Leader: The disciple Peter prayed and Tabitha came back to life.

Schooner: Her family and friends and neighbors dried their eyes and clapped for joy!

Leader: The miracle became known all over the city of Joppa and many came to believe in the Lord.

Schooner: Me too! Me too!

Leader: God's power helps us believe in him. In today's lesson we'll thank God for his amazing power. Bible 4U! up next.

1 Bible 4U!

Tabitha, a Christian woman, lived in the seacoast town of Joppa. She was a godly woman who helped the poor. She didn't just talk about doing good for others, she did good every day. She sewed clothes for others and helped the needy. Everyone loved Tabitha. Wouldn't you? When Tabitha died, her friends were heartbroken. Many of the poor women she had helped over the years gathered to support each other.

Word quickly spread of Tabitha's death. Friends and neighbors quickly sent for the disciple Peter who was only a few miles away in another town. We don't know what they expected of him, but people knew that Peter was a man of God and had performed miracles before. Peter had seen Jesus bring the dead back to life, so he knew God's power was stronger than death.

Today's Bible drama tells us how Peter's prayers brought a kind woman back to life.

Instant Prep

Select four girls to play the drama roles and give each girl a copy of "Tabitha Wakes Up" script to review.

for Overachievers

Have a drama team prepare the story. Dress everyone in Bibletime costumes. On one side of the stage, set up a table and chair for Mary, with paper and a feather for a quill. On the other side of the stage, set up Tabitha's sewing shop, with fabric draped on chairs and sewing supplies on a table.

"Tabitha, Wake Up!"

Based on Acts 9:36–42

On one side of stage, Mary sits and speaks aloud as she writes a letter. On the other side, actors dramatize events in Tabitha's shop.

Mary: Dear Esther, I'm sorry I haven't written for a while. One of the disciples is going to your city and promised to bring this letter to you. Since Papa drowned in the fishing boat accident, Mother and I have been taking care of the children and trying to make money for food and rent. But it's been hard. The only way we have made it so far is with the help of our Christian friend named Tabitha.

Across the stage, Tabitha sits sewing. Two other women enter.

Tabitha: Joannah! Abigail! I'm glad to see you.

Joannah: Good morning, Tabitha. We stopped by to thank you for the robes you made for us.

Abigail: *(sniffles softly)* No longer do I have a husband. All the widows in the town of Joppa feel the same way that I do—we don't know what we would do without you, Tabitha.

Tabitha: Thank you, Abigail. I'm using the gifts that the holy God gave me to help others.

Joannah: You're generous and kind. You bring food for our children, and make the most beautiful robes. And you charge us nothing.

Abigail: You shine the love of God in everyday ways. You are a blessing to the town.

Tabitha: *(hugs Abigail and Joannah)* I was just on my way to take this robe to Mary. Come along with me and keep me company. We'll talk as we walk.

Tabitha, Joannah and Abigail exit. Mary continues writing and speaking.

Mary: The wind off the sea is cold at night. The children sleep together in one bed, and Mother and I sleep on the dirt floor. But Tabitha does her best to keep us warm. She makes warm robes we can wrap in while we sleep. We're blessed to have Tabitha as one of the believers here in Joppa.

Across the stage, Joannah and Abigail enter, weeping.

Joannah: *(raises her hands to the sky)* Why did this happen? It can't be true! Tabitha was such a good person!

Abigail: *(wrings her hands)* I don't understand. It's not fair that she should get sick and die.

Joannah: Have you seen the crowds at her house?

Abigail: Yes, they washed Tabitha's body and placed it in an upstairs room until they can make arrangements to bury her.

Joannah: There must be something we can do.

Abigail: Her body is lifeless, Joannah. There is nothing we can do.

Joannah: Wait. I've heard of people coming back to life—by the power of the living God.

Abigail: Do you believe it? Do really think it could happen?

Joannah: *(excitedly)* Let's send for the disciple Peter. I've seen with my own eyes the miracle of his touch. God's power rests in him. Hurry. Peter is in the town of Lydda. That's only 12 miles from here. If he can get him here…

Abigail: *(wipes the tears from her eyes)* We have no time to waste.

Joannah and Abigail exit. Mary continues writing.

Mary: When the disciples heard that Tabitha had died, they sent two men to find Peter, the apostle. He wasn't far away. We were all sure he would want to help. But we weren't sure if he could help. Was it too late? But we were sure he would want to be with the believers who were grieving. And how happy we were when Peter did come, as soon as he heard. Quickly, he entered the room where Tabitha lay.

Joannah and Abigail enter.

Joannah: Did you see that? The whole room filled with weeping women. They wept over Tabitha. And each wore a beautiful robe that Tabitha had made.

Abigail: Peter wasted little time. He had them leave the room.

Joannah: This surprised me. But the women did as they were told.

Abigail: Peter believes in the power of the most high God.

Joannah: Abigail, do you believe in the power of God?

Abigail: I do. But standing in Tabitha's bedroom I wasn't sure what to believe. I hoped something great would happen, but how could I be sure?

Joannah: Peter got down on his knees and prayed.

Abigail: It seemed like such a simple thing.

Joannah: This I know to be true. God helps people who pray to him for help.

Joannah and Abigail exit. Mary continues writing.

Mary: We've seen proof of God's power! Why do we still doubt? Peter prayed, and then said, "Tabitha, get up." And Tabitha opened her eyes. When she saw Peter, she sat up. He took her by the hand and helped her to her feet.

Joannah, Abigail, and Tabitha enter.

Joannah: Tabitha! It's good to have you back with us. I can hardly believe it.

Abigail: When Peter called the believers and the widows together and showed us you were alive, I thought my heart would burst!

Tabitha: I'm happy that I can continue serving God and helping others.

They exit. Mary continues writing.

Mary: Esther, the power of God brought Tabitha back to life. When people in Joppa heard the news, many became Christians. I will never doubt the incredible power of God again. When we pray in Jesus' name, we pray in the power of the Ruler of heaven and earth. Share the story of this miracle with everyone in your town. Your sister in Christ, Mary.

All exit.

Bible 4U!

Nothing is impossible for God. Peter believed in the power of God and prayed for Tabitha to live again. God doesn't often choose to bring people back to life. Instead, we are called to trust in his wisdom. But never forget the awesome power available when we pray with faith, like Peter. Peter had seen the miracles Jesus did, so he knew firsthand the power of God. Let's see what you remember about God's power in our story.

Toss the four numbered balls to different parts of the room. Bring kids with the balls to the front one-by-one and ask these questions. Allow kids to get help from the group if they need it. After each correct answer, let kids drop the ball into a bag.

 ■ **Why did people love Tabitha?**

 ■ **What did Peter do when he heard Tabitha had died?**

 ■ **How did God use his power for Tabitha?**

 ■ **What was the reaction when the city of Joppa heard of Tabitha's new life?**

Let's talk about the miracles Peter had seen with his walk with Jesus. Share the following miracles with your group. The disciple Peter was there when Jesus brought back Jairus's daughter from the dead. Peter was there when Jesus gave life to the son of a widow who lived in Nain. Peter saw Jesus bring Lazarus back from the dead after Lazarus had been dead several days. Peter was there when Jesus fed a huge crowd with one boy's lunch. Peter knew Jesus died on the cross, but he saw him alive again several times before Jesus went back to heaven. Peter was there when the Holy Spirit came on the believers in Jerusalem. **Wow! So Peter knew a lot about God's power. He knew that God's power helps people who trust and believe in him. Peter trusted God to answer his prayer.**

Bible Verse
You are the God who performs miracles; you display your power among the peoples.
Psalm 77:14

As we spend time getting to know Jesus, our faith in the power of God grows too. We learn that God's power helps people believe in him, and when we believe, powerful things happen. Today in your shepherd groups, you'll learn about praying for God to show his power in our world today.

 *Dismiss kids to their shepherd groups.*

72

② Shepherd's Spot

Gather your small group and help kids find Acts 9:36–42 in their Bibles. Review the highlights of the story together.

■ **What might someone who didn't believe in God think after Tabitha's miracle?**

Never be afraid to pray. Pray for God to show you his power. Let's make a Power Pack to help us when we pray. Pass out the "Power Pack" handout. Once cut and folded, the "Power Pack" handout will form a small paper booklet. Have kids fold on the dashed lines to form eight sections to the page. Open the handout. Fold it in half the short way and cut on the dark solid line between the dots. Make sure to stop as indicated. Open the handout again and fold in half lengthwise. Hold the folded paper in front of you with the slit on top. Gently push in from the sides until the page folds into an eight page booklet. Fold and crease at the spine. Remind kids to fill in their names on the front. **Now you have your own Power Pack to help you remember that God's power is available to you through prayer.** Have a volunteer read Psalm 77:14 from page 3 of the handout: "You are the God who performs miracles; you display your power among the peoples."

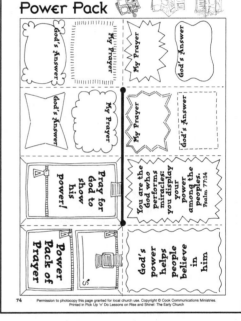

The death of someone we love makes us sad. God's love helps us. It doesn't take away all the hurt, but the power of God is there to comfort us when we pray.

Show kids the four pages inside the "Power Pack" where they can write what they're praying for. Then when God answers the prayer, they can record that also. If you'd like, have kids fill in the prayer spaces while you are together.

Let's pray for God to use his power to answer our prayers. Invite kids to share prayer concerns. Then pray together. **Dear Lord, thank you for loving us and for answering our prayers. We now pray silently for the things on our hearts today and ask you to show your power in times that are sad and stressful.** Pause for silent prayer. **Thank you for what you're going to do. Please walk beside our families this week. In Jesus' name we pray, amen.**

Power Pack

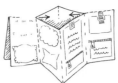

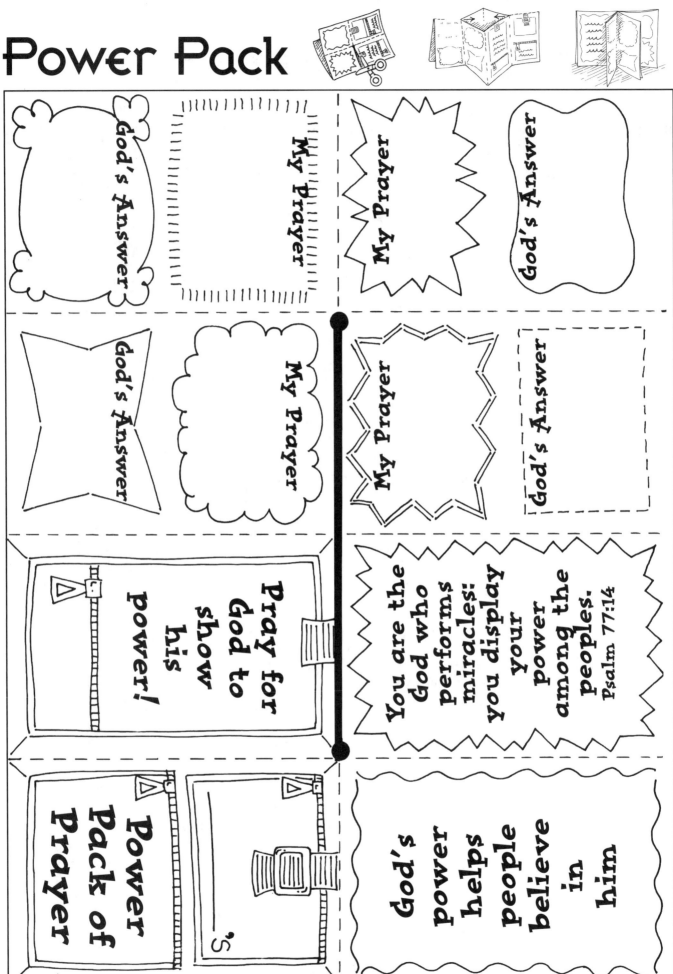

God's Answer

My Prayer

My Prayer

God's Answer

God's Answer

My Prayer

My Prayer

God's Answer

Pray for God to show his power!

You are the God who performs miracles; you display your power among the peoples. Psalm 77:14

Power Pack of Prayer

God's power helps people believe in him

Workshop Wonders*

Just imagine how happy and surprised the crowd was when Peter revealed Tabitha alive and well. Mourners had been sobbing uncontrollably when Peter arrived at Tabitha's home. Women spoke to Peter about all of the good and generous things Tabitha had done for them. By the time Peter left the house, however, shouts of joy could be heard throughout the whole city of Joppa. God showed his power by returning life to Tabitha, and through the miracle, the good news of Jesus was known far and wide.

Get List:
- flashlight with removable batteries

Optional:
- Wintergreen Lifesaver® candies
- hand mirrors

■ Tabitha was a well-loved Christian woman. How does kindness attract others?

■ How did the news of the miracle affect the people of Joppa?

Through God's power, people can see the light of the Gospel. God tells us he'll display his power in us and nothing is too hard for him. In prayer we go to God to receive a portion of his awesome power. Let's play a game that will shed some light on today's Bible truth.

Choose one child to be the "Seeker." Have a flashlight with its batteries removed on a table in front of the kids. Show everyone how to put the batteries in and how to turn the flashlight on. Then take the batteries out. The "Seeker" must close his or her eyes, while the rest hide, and the lights are turned out. Those hiding can sit very still and be unnoticed in the darkness. The seeker then opens his eyes, puts the batteries in, and turns on the flashlight. The seeker must find the "Lost" by standing still and shining the light around the room. When someone is found, the seeker calls the person to come to the light and sit down. Use a three-minute time limit to find everyone and choose another seeker. Adjust time to your situation.

Option: With the lights off, perform this simple experiment with your group. Pass out the Wintergreen Lifesaver candies, one per student. Have children look into mirrors as the smile and chew the candy. Watch! Sparkles of light appear as they chew. (This simple experiment demonstrates the mechanical generation of light.)

If your classroom in not dark enough and you are comfortable doing so, "reserve" a ladies restroom for this activity. Turn out the lights and have kids look into the large mirror as they chew. Caveat: Small candies can be choking hazards for young children so supervise carefully. Have water on hand for kids to drink.

We want to be God's light in the world, the way Tabitha was. Let's put in the batteries—God's Spirit—so we can shine brightly the light of God's love.

*Check with parents for any food allergies children may have.

Printed in Pick Up 'n' Do Lessons on Rise and Shine! The Early Church

Fold down the corners to start your paper airplane.

SPECIAL DELIVERY

TO

☆ Pray for God to show his power.

Here's a fun way to see what it might have felt like for Tabitha to come back to life. Play a game of Statues with your family or friends. Choose one person to be "It." The rest of the group moves around freely until "It" shouts "freeze." The group freezes instantly. Players should look like lifeless marble statues. The first person to move becomes the new "It." If no one moves, "It" shouts "Defrost!" and the game begins again. As fun as this game is, remember God's power is serious business. Pray for God to reveal it to you.

Today at church we learned that God's power helps people believe in him. □ Name someone you know who needs God's power. □ Tell about a time you saw God's power do something great.

Bible Verse

You are the God who performs miracles; you display your power among the peoples. Psalm 77:14

■ Where is your favorite place to pray?
■ Go to your favorite place and pray for God's power when you get home today.

☆ Family FUN ☆

Live It!

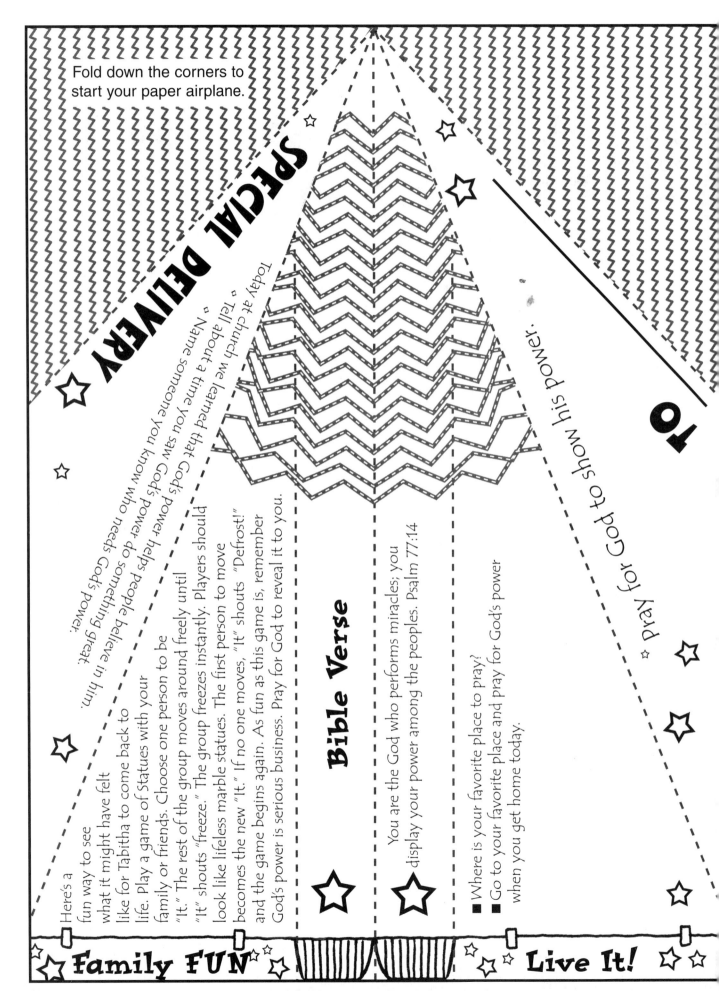

You're Welcome!

Option

Get Set
LARGE GROUP ■ Greet kids and do a puppet show. Schooner is not at all sure he wants to set out the welcome mat for all of God's children.
❑ *large bird puppet* ❑ *puppeteer*

1

Bible 4U! Instant Drama
LARGE GROUP ■ Roman Cornelius's son and daughter help tell the story of Peter's visit to Cornelius.
❑ *6 actors* ❑ *copies of pp. 80-81, "Everybody's Welcome" script*
❑ *4 numbered balls*   Optional: ❑ *Bibletime costumes, backdrop*

2

Shepherd's Spot
SMALL GROUP ■ Use the "All God's Children" handout to encourage kids to speak to others about God's love.
❑ *Bibles* ❑ *pencils* ❑ *scissors* ❑ *copies of p. 84, "All God's Children"*
❑ *copies of p. 86, Special Delivery*

Option

Workshop Wonders
SMALL GROUP ■ You're welcome! Play a game that lets everyone experience the great feeling of being welcomed.
❑ *small welcome mat*

Bible Basis
Peter meets a prayerful Cornelius. Acts 10:24–36, 44, 48

Learn It!
God's good news is for everyone.

Live It!
Welcome others into God's family.

Bible Verse
Yet to all who received him, to those who believed in his name, he gave the right to become children of God. John 1:12

Quick Takes

Acts 10:24-36, 44, 48

10:24 The following day he [Peter] arrived in Caesarea. Cornelius was expecting them and had called together his relatives and close friends. 25 As Peter entered the house, Cornelius met him and fell at his feet in reverence. 26 But Peter made him get up. "Stand up," he said, "I am only a man myself." 27 Talking with him, Peter went inside and found a large gathering of people. 28 He said to them: "You are well aware that it is against our law for a Jew to associate with a Gentile or visit him. But God has shown me that I should not call any man impure or unclean. 29 So when I was sent for, I came without raising any objection. May I ask why you sent for me?" 30 Cornelius answered: "Four days ago I was in my house praying at this hour, at three in the afternoon. Suddenly a man in shining clothes stood before me 31 and said, 'Cornelius, God has heard your prayer and remembered your gifts to the poor. 32 "Send to Joppa for Simon who is called Peter. He is a guest in the home of Simon the tanner, who lives by the sea.' 33 "So I sent for you immediately, and it was good of you to come. Now we are all here in the presence of God to listen to everything the Lord has commanded you to tell us." 34 Then Peter began to speak: "I now realize how true it is that God does not show favoritism 35 but accepts men from every nation who fear him and do what is right. 36 "You know the message God sent to the people of Israel, telling the good news of peace through Jesus Christ, who is Lord of all." 44 While Peter was still speaking these words, the Holy Spirit came on all who heard the message. 48 So he ordered that they be baptized in the name of Jesus Christ.

Insights

After praying and bringing Tabitha back to life, Peter stayed on in Joppa at the home of Simon the tanner. The work of a tanner involved contact with dead skins, which were unclean according to Jewish law. Peter's decision to stay with someone in regular contact with the unclean tells us he was already opening up to a broader interpretation of God's kingdom. While in Joppa, Peter had a vision in which the Lord told him it was all right to eat unclean foods. Just then, Gentile visitors from Caesarea arrived to ask Peter to go back with them to the home of Cornelius.

Cornelius was an officer in the Roman army, which did not exactly make him popular with the Jews. He was there in Caesarea to keep the peace, to quell any uprisings against Rome. But on a personal level, he also was seeking the true God. He probably worshiped at the temple and respected Jewish teachings, though he had not chosen to become a Jew. God gave Cornelius a vision to send for Peter.

Two visions came together when Peter crossed the threshold into Cornelius's house. In doing so, Peter broke a long list of Jewish rules. Imagine discovering that Cornelius had assembled an audience who had been waiting for Peter's arrival. What in the world was Peter getting into? But God had prepared Peter for this moment. Peter understood that the gospel was spreading beyond the Jews, that God welcomed all people into his kingdom. Peter helped Cornelius—and his household—go from fearing God to trusting Christ. The Holy Spirit came on everyone there, and Peter organized a baptismal service.

This changed the vision of the church. While Paul became the great missionary to the Gentiles, Peter, a critical figure among Jewish believers, also understood God's movement. The love of Jehovah God and Jesus Christ was for everyone. Use this lesson to teach that God's good news is for everyone.

Get Set

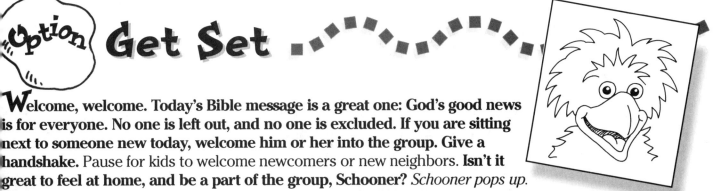

Welcome, welcome. Today's Bible message is a great one: God's good news is for everyone. No one is left out, and no one is excluded. If you are sitting next to someone new today, welcome him or her into the group. Give a handshake. Pause for kids to welcome newcomers or new neighbors. **Isn't it great to feel at home, and be a part of the group, Schooner?** *Schooner pops up.*

Schooner: Me, too, boss?

Leader: Of course, Schooner. We wouldn't think of leaving you out.

Schooner: I love to visit. I feel good when I come.

Leader: My prayer is that this is a place where all children feel that way. There's room for everybody in the family of God.

Schooner: But, boss, aren't there some who might not, you know, fit in?

Leader: Schooner, the whole point is that God accepts everyone with a heart for him.

Schooner: I mean some people might not be as holy as you and me. We go to church. We read our Bible stories. We're kind and generous. We're way up there on the holy scale! *Squawk!*

Leader: Only God can see the heart. What we do on the outside comes from how we love God on the inside.

Schooner: But people do really, really bad things.

Leader: Yes.

Schooner: People are mean.

Leader: Yes.

Schooner: Mean people don't belong. Not like us.

Leader: Nonetheless, we are to invite everyone to hear the Word of God. God changes hard hearts into soft and lovable hearts, remember Soul?

Schooner: But, what about people with bad taste?

Leader: *(shakes head)* What?

Schooner: People who like ketchup and pickle sandwiches. Yuck! God doesn't want them.

Leader: *(sternly)* Schooner, what did I say? God invites everyone into this family.

Schooner: *(ignores Leader)* What about people who sleep with their eyes open? Ewe. Scary.

Leader: *(rolls eyes)* Yes, they're included.

Schooner: What about people with purple hair or who wear neckties that spin and light up?

Leader: *(sighs)* Schooner, enough! You're a chatterbox today. Anyone who places trust and belief in Jesus becomes a child of God.

Schooner: *(giggles)* I like to tease you, boss. I get it. God wants everyone to come to him. And we're here to help.

Leader: The good news about God's love is…it doesn't leave anyone out.

Schooner: So…what's this have to do with our story today?

Leader: It was a lesson disciple Peter had to learn.

Schooner: Peter didn't know that?

Leader: In his time, it was against the law for a Jew to visit a Gentile.

Schooner: *(pause)* Um, what's a Gentile?

Leader: A Gentile is anyone who's not Jewish.

Schooner: Hey, I'm not Jewish!

Leader: You're not a Gentile either, Schooner. You're a parrot.

Schooner: *Squawk!* Right. So Peter was Jewish and he wanted to visit a Gentile. Did he go??

Leader: Yes. We'll meet Cornelius, a Roman Gentile, in today's Bible story.

Schooner: *(ponders)* You know, boss, you need courage to be a believer.

Leader: Yes, you do. Peter had a decision to make: Obey the Jewish law, or set out for the home of Cornelius who wanted to know more of God.

Schooner: Maybe it was a trap. Peter could be arrested.

Leader: Peter followed God's direction. The gospel calls for us to spread the Word and not just to people who look or think or act like us. God welcomes all people into his kingdom.

Schooner: *(fidgety)* So what happened?

Leader: Hold on to your tail feathers, Schooner. Bible 4U! coming up.

Printed in Pick Up 'n' Do Lessons on Rise and Shine!: The Early Church

1 Bible 4U!

Welcome to Bible 4U!. Let's do a little background before we start today's show. Since Jesus was a Jew, the love of God and the gift of Jesus' grace was, at first, shared only among the Jews. But when the high-ranking Jews and the Romans began to hurt the Jewish Christians, believers left Jerusalem and spread out among the Gentiles, people who weren't Jewish. God began to make it clear that his love and forgiveness was for all people.

Peter was one of Jesus' 12 disciples, and he became a powerful preacher after Jesus returned to heaven. Many people believed in Jesus because of Peter. Peter might have thought that he knew everything there was to know about Jesus and the good news. But even Peter had some lessons to learn. God wanted Peter to look beyond his culture and experience to see that the good news is for everyone.

Now, God got Peter's attention in an extra ordinary way—leading him to the home of a Roman soldier who wanted to know more about God. Let's get ready to listen to today's Bible drama, "Everybody's Welcome"!

Instant Prep
Assign six actors to play Peter, Cornelius, Son, Daughter and Narrators 1 and 2. Give each a copy of the "Everybody's Welcome" script to review.

for Overachievers
Have a drama team prepare the story. Provide Bibletime costumes and use furniture to make a set for Cornelius's house. Have one narrator stand on each side of the stage.

Everybody's Welcome
Based on Acts 10:24–36, 44, 48

Narrator 1: A Roman army soldier named Cornelius lived in Caesarea. He was in charge of 100 men. His job was to make sure no riots broke out and that people remained obedient to Roman law.

Narrator 2: Cornelius was not a Jew, but he prayed to God and tried to live a godly life. One day he was praying and an angel appeared to him. He told Cornelius to send a few men to get Peter. Peter came right away.

Peter enters opposite Cornelius's house.

Peter: Cornelius's house is not too far. It's just over in Caesarea, only about 12 miles from Joppa. I should be there soon.

(He begins walking across stage.)

Narrator 1: Meanwhile, back in Caesarea,

Cornelius was busy gathering his relatives and close friends. He wanted them to meet Peter.

Son and Daughter enter.

Son: Why do we have to get cleaned up anyway? Mom told me to put on my best tunic and get ready for company. Who's coming?

Daughter: Dad's invited Peter, the Jewish Christian who's been healing people and telling everyone about the risen Jesus. Friends and relatives will be here any minute to meet him too.

Son: Even Aunt Rose and Uncle Marcus?

Daughter: I'm afraid so.

Son: Are they bringing Cousin Justus?

Daughter: I'm afraid so.

Son: *(sighs)* We'll just have to make the best of

it. But why is the disciple Peter coming? Jews and Gentiles don't share their food or their homes.

Daughter: Dad believes in the one true God. Maybe he has questions that only Peter can answer.

Daughter: Hey, it sounds like everyone is here. Let's check it out.

They exit. Cornelius and Servant enter and stand in front of his home. Cornelius shades his eyes to watch the road.

Cornelius: *(looking down the road)* Peter should be here by now. Where is he? *(pointing)* There! There he is.

Peter arrives at Cornelius's house.

Cornelius: *(bowing to the ground in front of Peter)* Peter! Thank you, thank you for coming.

Peter: Please get up! I am not God, just a man like you.

Cornelius: *(gets up)* Come in and meet my family and friends. I want them all to hear about what you know of God and his Son, Jesus Christ.

They step into house area. Son and Daughter enter. Peter looks out at audience as if they are the crowd at Cornelius's house.

Narrator 1: Peter went into Cornelius's house and found Cornelius's friends and relatives there. The place was packed. Cornelius had invited everyone he knew. Guests were a little uneasy and wondered what Peter would say to them.

Peter: Wow! What a crowd.

Son: Dad's got half the city here.

Cornelius: Son, don't interrupt.

Peter: It's all right, Cornelius. Children ask questions that adults are often too afraid to ask.

Son: Is it really true that you brought the woman Tabitha back to life?

Daughter: And that you heal people who are blind or can't walk?

Peter: *(laughing)* So many questions. Come in and listen while I share my story.

Son: What will you talk about?

Peter: To start with, let me say it's against

Jewish law for me to be here. But God has shown me that his good news is for everyone. So when your father sent for me, I came right away, no questions asked. *(turns to Cornelius)* Thank you for welcoming me to your home, Cornelius. Now tell me what you want of me.

Cornelius: Peter, I've had a strange four days.

Son: That's for sure.

Daughter: Shhhh!

Cornelius: Four days ago I was here, in my house, praying at 3:00 in the afternoon.

Son: He does that every day.

Daughter: Shhhh!

Cornelius: Suddenly a man, an angel, in shining clothes stood in front of me.

Son: Dad freaked out!

Daughter: *(whispers loudly)* Will you please be quiet?

Cornelius: *(recalls the words he heard)* "Cornelius, send someone to Joppa to get Peter. He's staying at the home of Simon the tanner, by the sea." So I sent for you.

Son: And he's been waiting for you ever since.

Daughter: Shhhh!

Cornelius: I'm so glad you came. I've gathered everyone I know so we could all hear what you have to say.

Narrator 2: So Peter began to speak and tell the good news about Jesus.

Peter: God welcomes people from every nation, anyone who has respect for him and does what is right. The message that God sent to the people of Israel is for everyone. It's the news of peace through Jesus, the Lord of all.

Narrator 1: While Peter spoke, the Holy Spirit settled on everyone. Now they were all believers.

Narrator 2: Peter said, "Baptize all here in the name of Jesus!"

Narrator 1: God's good news message is for everyone.

Narrator 2: *(looks to the group)* Put out the Welcome mat and invite others to join God's family.

All exit.

The Bible tells us that anyone who receives Jesus becomes a child of God. God's love is for everyone. It's not a private club just for those who already believe. Everyone who is sorry for their sins and loves God belongs to God's family. We need to share the good news with friends and invite them to meet Jesus. What do you remember about our story?

Toss the four numbered balls to different parts of the room. Bring kids with the balls to the front one-by-one and ask these questions. Allow kids to get help from the group if they need it. After each correct answer, let kids drop the ball into a bag.

 ■ **At the beginning of the story, how did Cornelius show that he wanted to follow God?**

 ■ **Why did Cornelius send someone to get Peter?**

 ■ **What happened when Peter got to Cornelius's house?**

■ **Who can become part of God's family?**

Earlier in Scripture God gave Peter a vision to let him know it would be all right to go to Cornelius's house. And Cornelius had a vision that Peter would come. Cornelius sent someone to get Peter—because God told him to, and Peter went to Cornelius's house—because God told him to. God was busy communicating that day! Peter had learned that God wanted to welcome everyone into his family.

God's good news is for everyone. As we've learned, it's not just for people who already know God or come to church. No matter how different others may be from us, God's love is for them to enjoy too. God wants us to invite others into God's family. If God sends you to talk to a new friend, go, just like Peter did.

Bible Verse

Yet, to all who received him, to those who believed in his name, he gave the right to become children of God.
John 1:12

Today in your shepherd groups, you'll learn that you can welcome other people into God's family.

Dismiss kids to their shepherd groups.

2 Shepherd's Spot

Gather your small group and help kids find John 1:12 in their Bibles. Have a volunteer read the verse aloud.

If we are children of God that means we are forever part of God's family. He is our heavenly Father who loves us.

■ **According to this verse, how do we become part of God's family?**
■ **Who does God want to have as part of his family?**
■ **How can other people know how to become part of God's family?**

Peter was one of the very first missionaries to speak and share God's love with others. He and other missionaries spent their lives traveling around the world telling many cultures about Jesus Christ. Missionaries today invite people of all colors and countries to become part of God's family. But you don't have to be a missionary in a foreign country to invite someone to know Jesus.

Is that a surprise to you? Well, surprise! God's good news is for everyone, friends and family, those who are close to us. God wants us to welcome everyone into his family.

Let's make a stand-up reminder that God wants everyone to be part of his family. Pass out "All God's Children" handout. Follow the instructions to cut out the figures and fold to assemble.

When you take your handout home today, tell your family how God wants everyone to be part of his family. Tell them the good news that we can all be God's children. Let's pray for people we want to welcome into God's family. Invite kids to share prayer concerns, then pray. **Dear Lord, thank you for loving us. We pray for all the people who don't know that you love them.** Pause and have kids add names if desired. **Help us share your good news this week. Be with each of us until we come together again. In Jesus' name, amen.**

All God's Children

1. Cut strips apart on the solid lines.
2. Fold the strips in half and cut around the head shapes.
3. Fold the tabs forward, all in the same direction.

John 1:12

he gave the right to become children of God.

to those who believed in his name,

Yet, to all who received him,

4. Overlap the front tab of each piece with the back tab of the figure in front of it. Tape in place.
5. Finally, fold the final front tab under and tape in place. Your figures will now stand freely or nest closely.

84   Permission to photocopy this page granted for local church use. Copyright © Cook Communications Ministries.
Printed in Pick Up 'n' Do Lessons on Rise and Shine!: The Early Church

All God's Children

1. Cut strips apart on the solid lines.
2. Fold the strips in half and cut around the head shapes.
3. Fold the tabs forward, all in the same direction.

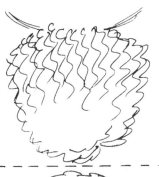

John 1:12

he gave the right to become children of God.

to those who believed in his name,

Yet, to all who received him,

4. Overlap the front tab of each piece with the back tab of the figure in front of it. Tape in place.
5. Finally, fold the final front tab under and tape in place. Your figures will now stand freely or nest closely.

Workshop Wonders

Peter walked into the house of Cornelius not knowing what to expect. All his life he had heard it was against Jewish law to visit with a Gentile. God wanted Peter to see with new eyes, and to accept with a new heart. What was "unclean" in the old days could no longer stop the sharing of the good news of Jesus. God does not show favoritism. God's good news is for everyone, and God welcomes everyone into his family.

Get List:
❑ small welcome mat

■ **What do you imagine Peter's thoughts were when he walked into the house filled with Cornelius' relatives and friends?**
■ **How does it feel to be welcomed somewhere new? How do you know when you're not welcomed in the playground at school or at a friend's house?**

Probably the last thing Peter expected was for Cornelius to fall at his feet in reverence! Peter told him to get up and began to share with them how to be in God's family.

Have kids sit in a game circle. Give the welcome mat to player #1. **The spot where you're sitting now is "home."** Practice the following couplet with the group, "Welcome, welcome, everyone. Welcome, welcome, home." **We'll pass the mat around the circle, passing it once for each word of our little game verse. If the mat lands "home" with you at the end of the verse, get up and trade places with any other player in the circle. We'll start the mat around again from your new position. Let's see how long it takes for players to return home, back to their original positions.**

Play until just before time runs out. See how many kids made it back to their original positions. Then gather kids to come, sit down, and talk about the experience.

■ **How did you feel when you're away from home for a while?**
■ **How did you feel when you return home and back into your own room?**

As much as we like to go out, most of us like to get home where we know our family loves and welcomes us. Others feel the same way.

■ **How do we show others that we welcome them into God's family?**

Isn't it wonderful to remember that God's promise in today's Bible verse is for everyone, which includes friends you will make in middle and high school, college and beyond! Repeat today's Bible verse with your group. "Yet, to all who received him, to those who believed in his name, he gave the right to become children of God" (John 1:12).

Fold down the corners to start your paper airplane.

SPECIAL DELIVERY

TO

Welcome everyone into God's family.

Today at church we learned that God's good news is for everyone to be part of God's family. "Name friends you know who need to become part of God's family." "How should we treat people who become part of God's family?"

Get some information from your church on missionaries your church supports. Pick ones that interest you. Find where they are on a world map. Start praying regularly for them and the people in the countries they live in. Write them a letter. Ask about the people there and ask for prayer requests. Surprise them with a care package.

Bible Verse

Yet, to all who received him, to those who believed in his name, he gave the right to become children of God. John 1:12

■ Remember that God loves you. Share his love with others.
■ Treat all people with love and respect even those who may look or dress differently or have customs that you are not familiar with.

Family FUN

Live It!

Keep Knocking Prayers

Option

Get Set
LARGE GROUP ■ Greet kids and do a puppet skit. Schooner hears of Peter's astounding escape from prison story.
❑ large bird puppet ❑ puppeteer

1

Bible 4U! Instant Drama
LARGE GROUP ■ Three angels relive the happenings of Peter's nighttime escape.
❑ 3 angel actors ❑ copies of pp. 90–91, "Broken Chains" script ❑ 4 numbered balls   Optional: ❑ 3 angel costumes ❑ table ❑ 3 chairs ❑ 3 coffee mugs ❑ cell phone ❑ paper chains

2

Shepherd's Spot
SMALL GROUP ■ Use the "Prayer Opens Doors" handout to help kids learn to pray with confidence. Share concerns and pray together. Send home the Special Delivery handout.
❑ Bibles ❑ pencils ❑ scissors ❑ copies of p. 94 "Prayer Opens Doors" ❑ copies of p. 96, Special Delivery

Option

Workshop Wonders
SMALL GROUP ■ Make unique slipknot wristbands as a reminder to give cares and worries to God.
❑ yarn cut in 1-yard lengths Optional: ❑ beads

Bible Basis
Peter escapes from prison. Acts 12:6–18

Learn It!
God answers prayer.

Live It!
Pray with confidence.

Bible Verse
Do not be anxious about anything, but in everything, by prayer and petition, with thanksgiving, present your requests to God. Philippians 4:6

Quick Takes

10:6 The night before Herod was to bring him to trial, Peter was sleeping between two soldiers, bound with two chains, and sentries stood guard at the entrance.
7 Suddenly an angel of the Lord appeared and a light shone in the cell. He struck Peter on the side and woke him up. "Quick, get up!" he said, and the chains fell off Peter's wrists.
8 Then the angel said to him, "Put on your clothes and sandals." And Peter did so. "Wrap your cloak around you and follow me," the angel told him.
9 Peter followed him out of the prison, but he had no idea that what the angel was doing was really happening; he thought he was seeing a vision.
10 They passed the first and second guards and came to the iron gate leading to the city. It opened for them by itself, and they went through it. When they had walked the length of one street, suddenly the angel left him.
11 Then Peter came to himself and said, "Now I know without a doubt that the Lord sent his angel and rescued me from Herod's clutches and from everything the Jewish people were anticipating."

12 When this had dawned on him, he went to the house of Mary the mother of John, also called Mark, where many people had gathered and were praying.
13 Peter knocked at the outer entrance, and a servant girl named Rhoda came to answer the door.
14 When she recognized Peter's voice, she was so overjoyed she ran back without opening it and exclaimed, "Peter is at the door!"
15 "You're out of your mind," they told her. When she kept insisting that it was so, they said, "It must be his angel."
16 But Peter kept on knocking, and when they opened the door and saw him, they were astonished.
17 Peter motioned with his hand for them to be quiet and described how the Lord had brought him out of prison. "Tell James and the other brothers about this," he said, and then he left for another place.
18 In the morning, there was no small commotion among the soldiers as to what had become of Peter.

Insights

Ten years have passed since the resurrection. The number of Christians in Jerusalem has swelled and become more and more of a problem for religious authorities. Herod Agrippa was in power at the time. He was the grandson of the Herod who tried to find and kill the infant Jesus, and the nephew of Herod Antipas, who beheaded John the Baptist. Christians have now been bothersome for three generations of Jewish rulers. Herod Agrippa executed James, the brother of John, and when this pleased the Jews, he went after Peter as well.

Peter's prison was probably a tower in one corner of the temple, the same place where Paul was later imprisoned. Prisons of the time were dark and harsh, crowded and overrunning with vermin. Peter was heavily guarded to ensure he would face trial.

While Peter was in prison, the church was "earnestly praying to God" for him. Yet, when he was released by the angel and knocked on the door where people were praying, at first no one but the servant girl believed it was him. They couldn't believe their prayers had really been answered. Their faith would allow them to speculate that Peter's angel was at the door, but not Peter himself. They couldn't believe God was really in control of the situation. Despite their prayers, they looked at the circumstances instead of at God.

Use this lesson to encourage kids to trust in God and not their circumstances. Teach them to pray with confidence in the all-powerful God who loves them.

Option Get Set

Hello and welcome. Today we'll learn about a miracle that frees the disciple Peter from a dark and dank prison. And it was nothing Peter did but God's power all along. *Schooner pops up.*

Schooner: Magicians on TV escape from handcuffs all the time, boss.

Leader: I remember reading about a famous escape artist who could get out of chains, straight jackets, prisons, and locked glass boxes filled with water.

Schooner: That's pretty amazing. How'd he do it?

Leader: No one really knows, Schooner. But he used tricks with mirrors and hidden keys, and his body was very flexible.

Schooner: I'm flexible, watch. *(tries to twist around)*

Leader: That's…um…well, pretty good.

Schooner: So our story is about tricks, huh?

Leader: No, not at all.

Schooner: Then why are we talking about tricks?

Leader: Today's Bible story is not a magician's trick.

Schooner: No tricks, huh. Booorrring!

Leader: You won't think it's boring when you hear what happened.

Schooner: *(confidently)* I'm a pretty bird, but I'm pretty hard to impress.

Leader: You, Mr. Parrot, will be totally impressed. It'll knock your socks off.

Schooner: I…

Leader: *(interrupts)* I know what you're going to say, Schooner. You don't wear socks.

Schooner: Right-e-o, boss!

Leader: The disciple Peter was arrested for preaching about Jesus. He was chained up in prison and guards stood watch.

Schooner: *(shakes head)* Poor Peter. *Squawk!*

Leader: The impressive part is this: Peter escaped!

Schooner: I thought you said there were no tricks in this story.

Leader: Not a single one.

Schooner: Peter must have had a hidden key.

Leader: *(shaking head)* No key.

Schooner: Peter had a spoon and he dug a tunnel under his bed.

Leader: *(shaking head)* No tunnel. He didn't even have a bed. He slept on the floor.

Schooner: *(excitedly)* Peter slipped by the guards, crawled out of the prison tower and found the keys swinging from a doorknob.

Leader: He was chained to the guards, Schooner.

Schooner: Mmm. This is a tough one.

Leader: Tough for you and me. Not tough for God.

Schooner: Peter must have had an accomplish.

Leader: An accomplish?

Schooner: You know, someone on the outside who helped him escape.

Leader: Oh, an accomplice. You're getting closer.

Schooner: Aha! Who was it? Was it another disciple?

Leader: No.

Schooner: Who? Who? Who? Who let Peter out?

Leader: God sent an angel to free Peter.

Schooner: Oh, I love angel stories. Such power! Such wonder! Such…power!

Leader: In a house not too far from the prison Peter's friends prayed night and day for his release. God answered their prayers.

Schooner: Totally cool!

Leader: God is an awesome God.

Schooner: Prayer is a powerful tool, boss.

Leader: Better than a cake with a saw baked inside! Story details in today's Bible 4U! Theater.

1 Bible 4U!

Welcome to Bible 4U! Theater. Never a dull moment in the Bible book of Acts! Seems like we have one amazing story after another, and sure enough, today's story is super amazing. Ten years had passed since Jesus rose back to heaven. The Christians faced bullying and persecution, but that didn't stop them from keeping the faith.

In today's story, Peter is in prison, chained to two soldiers. His trial is the next day. More than likely he will be killed for preaching about Jesus. But Peter's church friends are praying for him day and night. God answers their prayers by sending an angel on a special rescue mission. What a surprise! When Peter shows up at the house where his friends are praying, he knocks. But no one believes it is him.

Let's hear from three of God's angels, Gabe, Mikey, and Rafe, as they settle in at a coffee shop to discuss the prison breakout. When I give you this signal (choose a signal and demonstrate) shout, "No way! It can't be Peter!" Practice the signal and response. Let's listen to a little angel chit chat.

Instant Prep

Before class assign five volunteers to read the parts of the angels, Gabe, Mikey, and Rafe. Give each a copy of "Broken Chains" script so they can review their parts.

for Overachievers

Have a drama team prepare the story. Provide angel costumes, create a coffee shop set with a table, chairs, and mugs.

Broken Chains

Based on Acts 12:6–18

The three angels are drinking coffee.

Gabe: Mikey, stop doing loop-de-loops around the ceiling. *(sneezes)* You're stirring up the dust.

Mikey: Just shooting the breeze, Gabe. Got to keep in shape for the Lord's work. Hey, Gabe! That was fun last night.

Rafe: Prison gates are no match for an angel on a mission!

Gabe: Heaven was filled with prayers from Peter's friends and family. I could hear them in my sleep.

Mikey: Remind me. The guy who put Peter in jail is Herod Agrippa, right?

Rafe: I know this one! Herod Agrippa is the grandson of Herod the Great, the king who tried to kill the baby Jesus.

Gabe: Right, Rafe.

Mikey: Seems like that whole family is a bad bunch.

Gabe: Power has a way of making kings selfish and wicked.

Mikey: But Peter is such a nice guy. He preaches the love, kindness and miracles of Jesus. I can't imagine he'd do anything that deserves prison.

Leader gives signal to audience.

Audience: No way! It can't be Peter!

Rafe: Peter talked on how much he loved Jesus.

Gabe: *(sighs)* That's enough to get you in trouble these days. Peter was to go to trial this morning. I heard that Herod had already decided to execute him.

Mikey: *(makes a face)* Execute! Ewww! I don't like the sound of that.

Rafe: God's in charge, guys. He made sure it didn't happen.

Mikey: Did you see the look on Peter's face when Gabe shook him to wake him up? He looked like he'd just seen a ghost!

Gabe: Give Peter a break, guys. It was the middle of the night. Having a bright light shining in his face confused him.

Rafe: And when the chains fell off his wrists? That was a sight to see. The two soldiers he was chained to will have some explaining to do.

Mikey: *(laughing)* I like how he couldn't find his sandals.

Rafe: *(laughing)* And kept getting twisted in his robe.

Gabe: *(dismisses Mikey and Rafe)* Peter finally got dressed and we got out of there.

Mikey: The guards are sure in a pickle. How will they explain Peter walking through locked iron doors?

Leader gives signal to audience.

Audience: No way! It can't be Peter!

Rafe: Two sets of guards! You walked right past them.

Gabe: Peter thought the whole thing was a vision, a dream of some kind. Only later did he know it happened for real.

Mikey: *(laughing)* The best part…when we left Peter standing in the middle of the street. Poof, we were gone!

Gabe: *(sneezes)* I heard Peter before we left. He said, "Now I know without a doubt that the Lord sent his angel and rescued me from Herod's clutches."

Rafe: Good thing you didn't sneeze then, Gabe, or we'd have been found out for sure.

Gabe: Peter didn't waste a second running over to Mary's house.

Mikey: This just gets better and better. Peter knocks on the door, and Rhoda, the servant girl, hears his voice and freaks out.

Rafe: She can't believe it's him!

Leader gives signal to audience.

Audience: No way! It can't be Peter!

Mikey: She doesn't even open the door and let him in. She just goes screaming, "Hey, everybody, it's Peter!"

Rafe: So Peter's banging on the door saying, "It's me! Let me in!"

Mikey: And inside, everyone is telling Rhoda she's out of her mind. It can't be Peter.

Leader gives signal to audience.

Audience: No way! It can't be Peter!

Gabe: *(sneezes)* I don't know why they were surprised. After all, weren't they praying for Peter's release?

Rafe: God does big things. He's God!

Gabe: My point exactly.

Rafe: Well, my friends, what they lacked was "confidence."

Gabe: God answers prayers. Pray with confidence. Humans need to remember that.

Rafe: You said it, brother.

Gabe: Humans. They waste a lot of energy worrying about everything under the sun, instead of trusting God to take of things. When will they learn?

Mikey: *(laughs)* Meanwhile, Peter is still out there knocking and knocking. I love it.

Rafe: Finally somebody has the sense to open the door and let Peter in.

Gabe: Peter told of his amazing escape. All true, of course.

Mikey: I think it's time for us to get back to work.

Gabe: *(sneezes)* Don't stir up the dust this time. I'm running out of tissues.

Rafe: *(looks at the audience)* God's answers prayer. Remember to pray with everything you've got!

Bible 4U!

Peter had little idea what life would be like once he accepted Jesus into his heart. No doubt, it was an adventure! He never knew what was going to happen next. God did many miracles in and through Peter's life. Having an angel break him out of a prison was one of those miracles. See what you can remember about Peter's prison experience.

Toss the four numbered balls to different parts of the room. Bring kids with the balls to the front one-by-one and ask these questions. Allow kids to get help from the group if they need it. After each correct answer, let kids drop the ball into a bag.

 ■ Why was Peter in prison in the first place?

 ■ What did his friends do while Peter was in prison?

 ■ How did Peter get out of prison?

 ■ What did his prayer friends do when they discovered Peter was out of prison?

The God who created the universe cares for each of us and listens to our prayers. He may not always answer in a dramatic way like he did with Peter, but we can pray with confidence that God answers prayer.

Does that mean that God always gives us whatever we want? Do your parents always give you what you ask for? No, because they want what is best for you. God gives us what is best for us. And that's not always the way we want things to turn out.

When you pray, talk like you would to a friend or a parent. You don't need fancy words. You can pray with our eyes open or closed. People pray with their eyes closed because it helps them concentrate on God and not on what's going on around us. However you like to pray, stay one step ahead of Peter's friends. Expect God to answer your prayers! Expect God to do something! That's what praying with confidence is all about.

Bible Verse
"Do not be anxious about anything, but in everything, by prayer and petition, with thanksgiving, present your requests to God. Philippians 4:6

Today in your shepherd groups, you'll find out that we can always pray with confidence because the Bible says God always listens and answers our prayers.

Dismiss kids to their shepherd groups.

92

2 Shepherd's Spot

Gather your small group and help kids find Philippians 4:6 in their Bibles.

It's hard to understand why bad things happen to those that love Jesus. Prison was an awful place in Bible times. There was little light, no beds, rats, and bugs, and what little food the prisoners had needed to be shared. Yet Peter loved God despite the hardship.

Have a volunteer read Philippians 4:6 aloud.

■ According to this verse, what should we pray about?

■ What should our attitude be when we pray? Is prayer always about asking for things? Should praises be part of prayer?

■ What are some of the things you pray about? What did it feel like to have your prayer answered?

God asks us to worship and trust him even when we are uncomfortable, hurting, and unsure of what tomorrow will bring. If we have a problem to pray about, it helps to think about how big God is and how small the problem is compared to God. The friends praying for Peter were scared he would be killed. But God is bigger than earthly problems. If God had not chosen to save Peter, Peter would have gone to heaven to be with God. His family and friends would have missed him but Peter would be living joyously with Jesus.

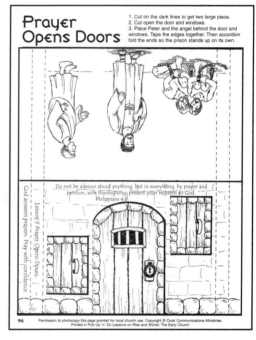

If you find that you can't stop worrying about something, pray about it. Talk with an adult who cares about you. Sometimes it helps to pray with another person you trust. No problem is too big for God to handle. No problem that worries you is too small to pray about. God listens to our prayers.

Let's make a reminder to pray with confidence because God answers our prayers.

Pass out the "Prayer Opens Doors" handout. Have kids cut, color and fold to assemble. Have volunteers read the verses.

When you take your handout home today, use it to remind you to pray. Invite kids to share prayer concerns, then pray together. **Dear Lord, thank you for listening to our prayers. We pray for all the people who are sick or hurting or sad today.** Pray about kids' concerns. **Help us to pray instead of worry. In Jesus' name, amen.**

Prayer Opens Doors

1. Cut on the dark lines to get two large piece.
2. Cut open the door and windows.
3. Place Peter and the angel behind the door and windows. Tape the edges together. Then accordion fold the ends so the prison stands up on its own.

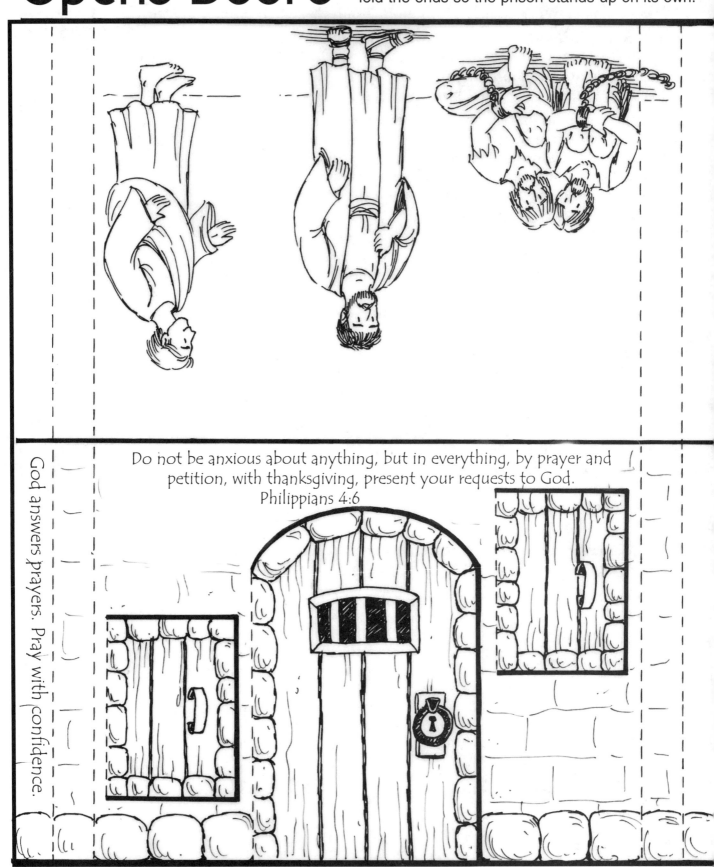

Do not be anxious about anything, but in everything, by prayer and petition, with thanksgiving, present your requests to God.
Philippians 4:6

God answers prayers. Pray with confidence.

94

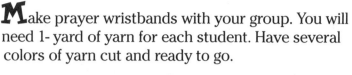

Make prayer wristbands with your group. You will need 1-yard of yarn for each student. Have several colors of yarn cut and ready to go.

Get List:
- ❑ yarn cut in 1-yard lengths
- ❑ Optional: beads

Peter lies fast asleep between two guards. The angel appeared and gave him a good poke to wake him up. Scripture tells us that Peter thought his rescue a vision, something he was dreaming about. Peter experienced unusual happenings that night. But he trusted in God. He didn't allow his fears of prison or an angel rescue to overwhelm him.

Our Bible verse today tells us not to be anxious about anything. Read Philippians 4:6 from a Bible: "Do not be anxious about anything, but in everything, by prayer and petition, with thanksgiving, present your requests to God."

- ■ **What kinds of things make you anxious?**
- ■ **How can praying about these things help? How can others praying help too?**

Our Bible verse says that we don't have to live in fear. "Petition" means asking. We ask God to give us what we need. We're thankful because we know without doubt that he'll take care of us.

Prayer brought an angel to break Peter's chains. Fear and worry are chains in our lives. I have an interesting way for us to remember that God can break fear's chains. We'll begin with a length of yarn. Select yarn and work alongside your kids.

Fear erases joy and hope. Like the chains that Peter wore in prison, anxious thoughts tie us down and keep us from doing the will of God. **Let's name a few things that get us knotted up from time to time.** For each fear or worry mentioned, make a slipknot with the yarn. (See illustrations.) Before long you should have a chain of knots. **Worry chains us to fear and fear to doubt and doubt to gloom and so on and so on. Now, let's give these worries to God and allow him to release the chains.** Pull on the ends of the yarn gently and the knots pull apart.

Start the slipknot process again. This time have kids make a series of slipknots to form a wristband. Secure loose ends with a colorful bead before knotting. Suggest that kids make several bands to wear.

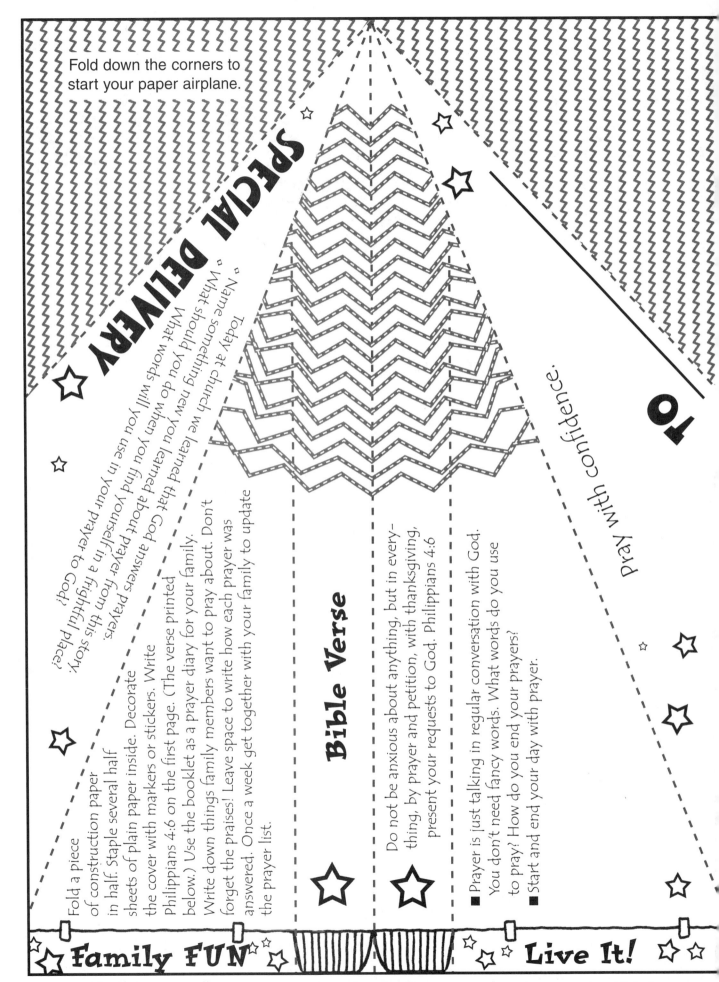

Fold down the corners to start your paper airplane.

SPECIAL DELIVERY

TO

Pray with confidence.

Bible Verse

"Name something new you learned about prayer from this story. What should you do when you find yourself in a frightful place? What words will you use in your prayer to God?"

Today at church we learned that God answers prayers.

Fold a piece of construction paper in half. Staple several half sheets of plain paper inside. Decorate the cover with markers or stickers. Write Philippians 4:6 on the first page. (The verse printed below.) Use the booklet as a prayer diary for your family. Write down things family members want to pray about. Don't forget the praises! Leave space to write how each prayer was answered. Once a week get together with your family to update the prayer list.

Do not be anxious about anything, but in every-thing, by prayer and petition, with thanksgiving, present your requests to God. Philippians 4:6

■ Prayer is just talking in regular conversation with God. You don't need fancy words. What words do you use to pray? How do you end your prayers?
■ Start and end your day with prayer.

☆ Family FUN

Live It!

Choose Joy

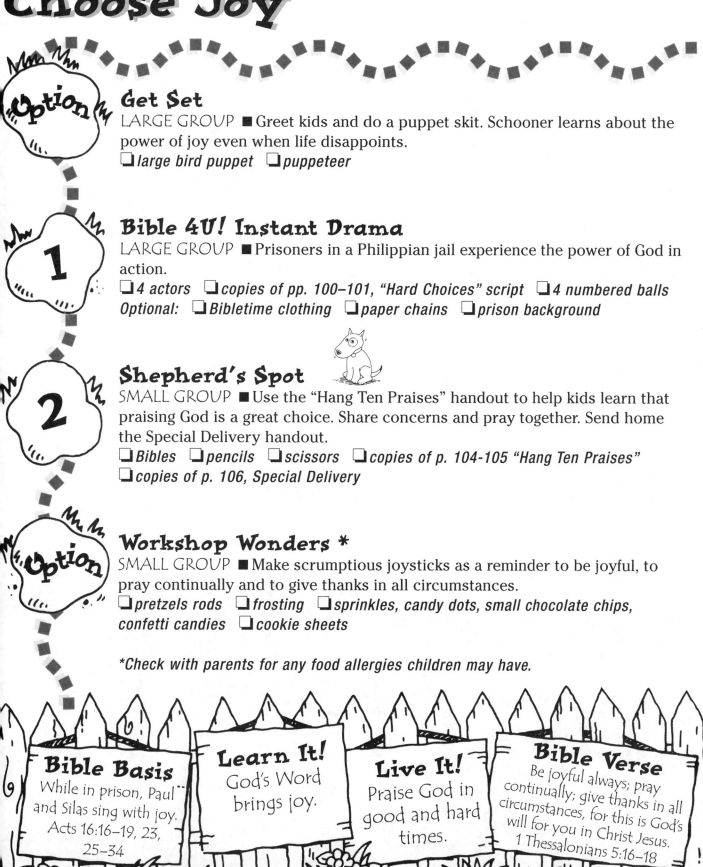

Option

Get Set
LARGE GROUP ■ Greet kids and do a puppet skit. Schooner learns about the power of joy even when life disappoints.
❏ *large bird puppet* ❏ *puppeteer*

1

Bible 4U! Instant Drama
LARGE GROUP ■ Prisoners in a Philippian jail experience the power of God in action.
❏ *4 actors* ❏ *copies of pp. 100–101, "Hard Choices" script* ❏ *4 numbered balls*
Optional: ❏ *Bibletime clothing* ❏ *paper chains* ❏ *prison background*

2

Shepherd's Spot
SMALL GROUP ■ Use the "Hang Ten Praises" handout to help kids learn that praising God is a great choice. Share concerns and pray together. Send home the Special Delivery handout.
❏ *Bibles* ❏ *pencils* ❏ *scissors* ❏ *copies of p. 104-105 "Hang Ten Praises"*
❏ *copies of p. 106, Special Delivery*

Option

Workshop Wonders *
SMALL GROUP ■ Make scrumptious joysticks as a reminder to be joyful, to pray continually and to give thanks in all circumstances.
❏ *pretzels rods* ❏ *frosting* ❏ *sprinkles, candy dots, small chocolate chips, confetti candies* ❏ *cookie sheets*

*Check with parents for any food allergies children may have.

Bible Basis
While in prison, Paul and Silas sing with joy.
Acts 16:16–19, 23, 25–34

Learn It!
God's Word brings joy.

Live It!
Praise God in good and hard times.

Bible Verse
Be joyful always; pray continually; give thanks in all circumstances, for this is God's will for you in Christ Jesus.
1 Thessalonians 5:16–18

Quick Takes

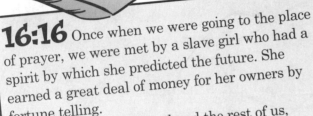

Acts 16:16–19, 23, 25–34

16:16 Once when we were going to the place of prayer, we were met by a slave girl who had a spirit by which she predicted the future. She earned a great deal of money for her owners by fortune telling.
17 This girl followed Paul and the rest of us, shouting, "These men are servants of the Most High God, who are telling you the way to be saved."
18 She kept this up for many days. Finally Paul became so troubled that he turned round and said to the spirit, "In the name of Jesus Christ I command you to come out of her!" At that moment the spirit left her.
19 When the owners of the slave girl realized that their hope of making money was gone, they seized Paul and Silas and dragged them into the market place to face the authorities.
23 After they had been severely flogged, they were thrown into prison, and the jailer was commanded to guard them carefully.
25 About midnight Paul and Silas were praying and singing hymns to God, and the other prisoners were listening to them.

26 Suddenly there was such a violent earthquake that the foundations of the prison were shaken. At once all the prison doors flew open, and everybody's chains came loose.
27 The jailer woke up, and when he saw the prison doors open, he drew his sword and was about to kill himself because he thought the prisoners had escaped.
28 But Paul shouted, "Don't harm yourself! We are all here!"
29 The jailer called for lights, rushed in and fell trembling before Paul and Silas.
30 He then brought them out and asked, "Sirs, what must I do to be saved?"
31 They replied, "Believe in the Lord Jesus, and you will be saved—you and your household."
32 Then they spoke the word of the Lord to him and to all the others in his house.
33 At that hour of the night the jailer took them and washed their wounds; then immediately he and all his family were baptized.
34 The jailer brought them into his house and set a meal before them; he was filled with joy because he had come to believe in God—he and his whole family.

Insights

As he travels, Saul is now known more and more by the Latin form of his name, Paul. Silas is accompanying Paul on his missionary journey, and in Derbe Paul invites Timothy to join them (16:3). Since Luke uses the word "we" in this section, we know that he is with Paul as well. Luke probably joined Paul in Troas (16:11).

Fortune telling was not unusual at this time, often accomplished by superstitious techniques. The slave girl in this story had an evil spirit that caused her to interpret signs and blurt out the future, and her owners were making a significant amount of money off of her. We don't know how accurate she was, but we do know that she was speaking the truth about Paul and Silas. If she's telling the truth, what's the problem, we might ask? Paul adamantly did not want the gospel linked with the activity of an evil spirit. Rather than encouraging people to accept the gospel,

this association would damage his ministry.

Paul and Silas are jailed on false charges to get them off the streets, but they don't seem bothered much by their circumstances. Obviously they've had a hard day. But at midnight they are awake and praying and singing hymns. The other prisoners were listening—Paul never misses a chance to evangelize!

When the earthquake throws open the prison doors, the jailer is ready to kill himself; he knows he will soon be killed anyway for failing his duties. But Paul and Silas and all the other prisoners stay right where they are, opening yet another door joyfully to spread the word about Jesus.

Use today's lesson to encourage children to be joyful and look for ways to pray and praise God in all circumstances.

Option Get Set

Welcome. I'm glad you've come. Feelings go every which way, don't they? Happy and sad. Mad and glad. Being a Christian is like being right side up in an upside-down world. We want to do right, but the world doesn't make it easy. Schooner, come up and say hello. *Schooner pops up.*

Schooner: Hello. *Squawk!* What are we going to do today, boss, stand on our heads?

Leader: No, but we'll think about how to change the way we act, when others treat us badly.

Schooner: *Squawk!* I know how I react.

Leader: Why don't you tell us?

Schooner: I get mad and flap my wings. *(flaps wings)*

Leader: That's how most people react, except for the wing part.

Schooner: Well, can you blame them?

Leader: Yes and no.

Schooner: Make up your mind, boss.

Leader: Maybe I should explain myself.

Schooner: This should be good. *Squawk!*

Leader: Shall I start with yes or with no?

Schooner: Start with no.

Leader: I know what it feels like to be disappointed and hurt by others.

Schooner: *(bows head)* Me too, boss

Leader: It's part of our nature to feel that way.

Schooner: *(brightens up)* I like nature. Grass, meadows, trees, mountains, pretty animals…

Leader: Oh, sorry Schooner. I mean how people are made. Our feelings.

Schooner: So what about the yes part?

Leader: Even though we feel disappointment and anger, we can be joyful.

Schooner: Noooo way.

Leader: Yes way.

Schooner: I'm going to need more convincing.

Leader: How about an example from the Bible?

Schooner: I can't argue with that.

Leader: Today's story tells us of the early church missionaries Paul and Silas.

Schooner: Oh, Saul-Paul! Spreading the Word of God.

Leader: He's the one. And, of course, Silas.

Schooner: How did they get disappointed?

Leader: They were jailed for helping a young girl.

Schooner: Put in jail…like the disciple Peter in last week's story! Major bummer. Did they rant and rave and shake their angry fists?

Leader: No.

Schooner: Bang the walls and yell at the guard? Call a lawyer?

Leader: No, none of that.

Schooner: What did they do?

Leader: They sang.

Schooner: Excuse me?

Leader: They sang.

Schooner: *(clears throat and sings)* "Poor, poor me, I'm sad and grumpy."

Leader: Schooner…they sang praises to God.

Schooner: *Squawk!* But that's nuts. They were in prison!

Leader: And both Paul and Silas had been whipped before being dragged to prison. Still, they sang hymns of joy and prayed in thanksgiving.

Schooner: *(pleading)* That's upside-down, boss.

Leader: Just like our upside-down Bible verse for today. Be joyful always.

Schooner: Always?

Leader: Pray continually.

Schooner: Hmm.

Leader: And give thanks in all circumstances.

Schooner: Even in prison? This is hard stuff, boss.

Leader: It is, Schooner. But like last week's story, this one has an exciting hard-to-believe ending.

Schooner: Oh good, I like super-stories like that.

Leader: Bible 4U! coming on through.

1 Bible 4U!

Welcome to Bible 4U! Theater! In Acts 16, we find Paul traveling. This story occurs during the second big trip that Paul took to tell people about Jesus. Friends have joined him. Luke and Timothy are with him, and Silas is helping him preach in the cities they visited.

Paul and Silas had an opportunity to preach with their actions, not just with their words. When they were treated unfairly and went to jail, they could have easily become discouraged. But they didn't. Even in jail, chained with a guard watching them, they looked for ways to praise God.

Instant Prep

Before class assign five volunteers to read the parts of Paul, Silas, two prisoners, and jailer. Give each a copy of the "Hard Choices" script to review.

for Overachievers

Have a drama team prepare the story. Create a prison set with scattered boxes and Bibletime clothing. Hang strips of crepe paper from the ceiling to create the appearance of cell bars. Use paper chains to connect all four prisoners together or chain them all to a fixed object. Give the jailer a flashlight and sword.

Our story has an earthquake in it. When I give the signal (demonstrate a signal of your choice), **stamp your feet and slap your knees. When I give the signal again, the earthquake is over.** Practice the signal and response.

Get ready to listen and quake!

Hard Choices
Based on Acts 16:16-19, 23, 25-34

Prisoner 1: I hate being a prisoner in this crummy Roman jail. All I did was steal two pigs and a chicken from my neighbor. He'll never miss them. I hate this place. No bed, no fresh air. It stinks.

Prisoner 2: The jailer is mean, the guards are nasty, and the food is watery soup and hard bread if we get fed at all.

Prisoner 1: *(looking over at Paul and Silas, who are humming)* What's the story with the new guys?

Prisoner 2: I don't know. They don't talk much.

Prisoner 1: They sure sing a lot, though. And they've been praying all day.

Prisoner 2: Hey, you! You happy guys! What's the deal?

Prisoner 1: Why are you here?

Paul: I don't know yet, but I'm sure God has a purpose.

Prisoner 2: What kind of answer is that?

Silas: *(to Paul)* I think he wants to know what crime we committed.

Paul: But we didn't commit a crime.

Silas: Maybe we should share our story.

Paul: *(nods in agreement)* In the city of Philippi we preached about the power and love of Jesus.

Silas: A slave girl started following us. She was a fortune teller.

Prisoner 1: I know the girl. Her owners make a lot of money with her fortune telling.

Paul: I'm afraid they won't make any more money.

Prisoner 2: What did you do? Kill her?

Silas: Of course not. Paul healed her.

Prisoner 1: Healed her?

Paul: (*recalls the girl's words*) "These men are servants of the Most High God, who are telling you the way to be saved." This is what she shouted again and again, day after day.

Prisoner 2: I don't see the problem guys. You *are* servants of God.

Silas: Yes, but the message sounded false coming from a fortune teller.

Paul: I shouted to her with all the power I could, "In the name of Jesus Christ, I command you to come out of her!"

Prisoner 1: Let me guess. The spirit left her, and now she couldn't tell the future anymore?

Silas: That's it.

Prisoner 2: Man, oh man! Her owners must have been mad as hornets!

Paul: We were accused us of stirring up a riot in the city.

Silas: And that's how we ended up here.

Prisoner 1: Why aren't you more upset? You're singing…in a prison!

Prisoner 2: (*strains neck to look at the arms of Paul and Silas*) Looks to me like you got a pretty good beating too.

Paul: God has a purpose for everything. I praise God wherever I find myself.

Prisoner 1: You're in an awful jail and your arms are bleeding. What has God done for you lately?

Silas: I will tell you. God has saved our souls and he'll take us to live in heaven with him someday.

Paul: He's forgiven all our sins and given us the Holy Spirit.

Prisoner 2: That's all fine and good. But it's almost midnight and I need my sleep. No…more…singing.

Prisoner 1: (*starts swaying*) Hey! What's going on? The floor is shaking. The jail is shaking!

Leader gives signals for audience to start and stop earthquake noise. All prisoners break their chains apart.

Prisoner 2: An earthquake! And we're still alive! The doors are open and our chains have broken off. Let's get out of here. (*gets ready to run*)

Paul: Stay right where you are! No one is leaving.

Prisoners 1 and 2: What?

Silas: You heard the man.

Jailer enters with flashlight.

Jailer: Oh no! Where are the prisoners? The Roman captain will kill me for letting them escape. I'll take my own life before he finds me. (*pulls sword*)

Silas: Stop!

Paul: Don't hurt yourself. We're still here.

Jailer: But the doors are wide open, and all your chains are loose.

Paul: We're still here.

Jailer: (*falls at Paul's feet*) I know you are a godly man. You talk about Jesus wherever you go. Please, tell me what I should do to be saved?

Paul: This is the good news. Jesus loves you and died for your sins. It's your choice. Believe in the Lord Jesus and you will be saved.

Jailer: (*joyfully*) I do believe. Come home with me. I will wash your wounds and my wife will prepare a hearty meal.

Paul: And after I will baptize you and your family.

Jailer: Praise the Almighty God for this joyful day!

All three exit, humming a joyful hymn.

The more we understand God's love for us, the more joy we have. We praise God no matter what life is like. That's what Paul and Silas show us in today's story. Even though both had been badly hurt and thrown into prison, they chose to be joyful. Sounds impossible? It's not. God wants us to be joyful and give thanks no matter where we find ourselves.

Toss the four numbered balls to different parts of the room. Bring kids with the balls to the front one-by-one and ask these questions. Allow kids to get help from the group if they need it. After each correct answer, let kids drop the ball into a bag.

■ Why were Paul and Silas in prison?

■ What did Paul and Silas do when the earthquake hit?

■ What did the jailer do after he became a Christian? Was he feeling mad, glad, sad or joyful?

■ What is one joy-thing you learned from today's story that you can share with your family at home?

Paul and Silas had the choice to preach or to stay silent about Jesus. They had the choice to help the young girl or do nothing. They had the choice to praise God and be joyful when things were hard or to complain. We have choices too. We can thank God throughout the day and pray so that we stay connected to him.

God asks you to praise him in all times. Trust in him. You will face choices but you won't face them alone. Our wise God wants you to be joyful, and his Holy Spirit helps you do it.

Today in your shepherd groups, you'll find out how we can praise God and pray and be joyful.

Dismiss kids to their shepherd groups.

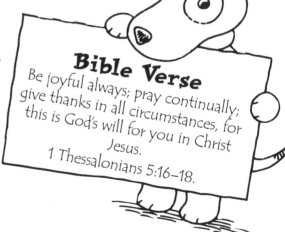

Bible Verse
Be joyful always; pray continually; give thanks in all circumstances, for this is God's will for you in Christ Jesus.
1 Thessalonians 5:16–18.

② Shepherd's Spot

Gather your small group and help kids find 1 Thessalonians 5:16–18 in their Bibles.

Paul and Silas spent their time in a prison praying and singing. When things go wrong, it doesn't help to blame someone or get mad or grumble and complain. Even though there may be things that we can't change, there is always one thing we can change. That's the way we act. Choose joy over anger, joy over harsh words, joy over complaining. Our Bible verse has great instructions from God on how we should live.

Have a volunteer read 1 Thessalonians 5:16–18 aloud. "Be joyful always; pray continually; give thanks in all circumstances, for this is God's will for you in Christ Jesus."

- ■ What things do you grumble about the most? How does your choice to grumble and complain affect your family? Your friends?
- ■ What attitude does God want you to have, instead of grumbling?

Let's make a reminder of 10 things we can praise God for. Pass out the "Hang Ten Praises" handout. Have kids cut the hanger out on the bold lines. Cut in and cut the circle to make the doorknob hole. Ask kids to write or print ten things they can praise God for such as family, grandparents, friends, love, life, fresh food, the joy of books and sports and dance and music. Invite volunteers to read their praises.

When you get home, hang your handout on your bedroom doorknob so you'll see it everyday. Let's pray for people who need to know that God loves them so they can be joyful too. Invite kids to share prayer concerns, then pray together. **Dear Lord, thank you for loving and protecting us. We pray for all the people who don't know that you love them. Help us to be thankful no matter how the day goes. After all, tomorrow is another bright and beautiful day in your world.** Pause and have kids pray if you wish. **Make us joyful for the wonderful things you give us every day. In Jesus' name, amen.**

Hang Ten Praises

1. Cut out the door-hanger on the solid lines. Color if desired.
2. Cut into the circle on the cut line that begins at the outside edge. Cut out the circle.
3. Write down ten things you can thank God for. Remember to praise God no matter what.
4. Hang the Hang Ten Praises on your bedroom door.

Hang Ten Praises

1.
2.
3.
4.
5.
6.
7.
8.
9.
10.

Be joyful always; pray continually; give thanks in all circumstances, for this is God's will for you in Christ Jesus.
1 Thessalonians 5:16–18

Hang Ten Praises

1. Cut out the door-hanger on the solid lines. Color if desired.
2. Cut into the circle on the cut line that begins at the outside edge. Cut out the circle.
3. Write down 10 things you can thank God for. Remember to praise God no matter what.
4. Hang the Hang Ten Praises on your bedroom door.

Hang Ten Praises

1. _____
2. _____
3. _____
4. _____
5. _____
6. _____
7. _____
8. _____
9. _____
10. _____

Be joyful always; pray continually; give thanks in all circumstances, for this is God's will for you in Christ Jesus.
1 Thessalonians 5:16–18

Workshop Wonders*

Paul and Silas were in a sad place—prison. The did not have freedom to come and go as they pleased. They had been hurt and thrown in prison all because they showed kindness to a troubled young girl.

■ You try to do the right thing and it turns out bad. Have you ever had that happen to you?

The future seemed pretty dark and hopeless for Paul and Silas. But instead of crying, they cried out in joyful song!

■ If you were one of the other prisoners in that jail, what would you think of Paul and Silas? Would you want to know the source of their joy?

Paul and Silas responded in faith by praising God. God responded by helping them in an amazing way.

■ How did God help Paul and Silas?
■ Why didn't Paul and Silas take advantage of the earthquake and run away? How would that have hurt the Jailer and his family?

Ask a volunteer to read 1 Thessalonians 5:16–18 aloud: "Be joyful always; pray continually; give thanks in all circumstances, for this is God's will for you in Christ Jesus."

■ According to these Scripture verses, what attitude does God want us to have in good times? In hard times?

Tell your group that a joystick is the way to control the pointer in video games. (This many of them will know!) Explain that the original meaning came from the main control stick in a small airplane. **The pilot moves the stick in a variety of directions in order to control the plane. The pilot judges which way to move the joystick according to what he wants the plane to do. Let's make joysticks we can snack on to remind us that no matter which way the winds of life toss us, we are to be joyful in praising God.**

Pass out pretzel rods. Set out tubs of frosting and scatter the sprinkles on a flat cookie sheets.

■ If the pretzel stick represents joy, what could the frosting and sprinkles represent?

Cover half of the pretzel in frosting. Roll the frosted end in the sprinkles. Remind kids that after they bite the end of the pretzel they may not put it back in the frosting or sprinkles.

*Check with parents for any food allergies children may have.

Fold down the corners to start your paper airplane.

SPECIAL DELIVERY

TO

Praise God in good and hard times.

☆ *Praise God in good and hard times.*

Today at church we learned that Paul and Silas prayed, sang and were joyful in prison. The Bible verse says to pray continually. How can you do that? Name two things you can thank God for every day.

Family FUN

Sit in a circle with your family. Go through the alphabet naming something to be thankful for. The first person names something that begins with the letter A. The second person names something that begins with the letter B. See how long it takes you to come up with 26 things to thank God for! To make this more challenging, have each person repeat all the letters and items already named before adding the next letter. Who can remember all 26? Help each other out if someone gets stuck.

Bible Verse

Be joyful always; pray continually; give thanks in all circumstances, for this is God's will for you in Christ Jesus. 1 Thessalonians 5:16-18

Live It!

■ Count off! Hold up your hand and name a good thing for each finger. Thank God for each.

■ If you have a bad day, ask God to help you be joyful. The Holy Spirit is your helper and he will help you when you can't go it alone.

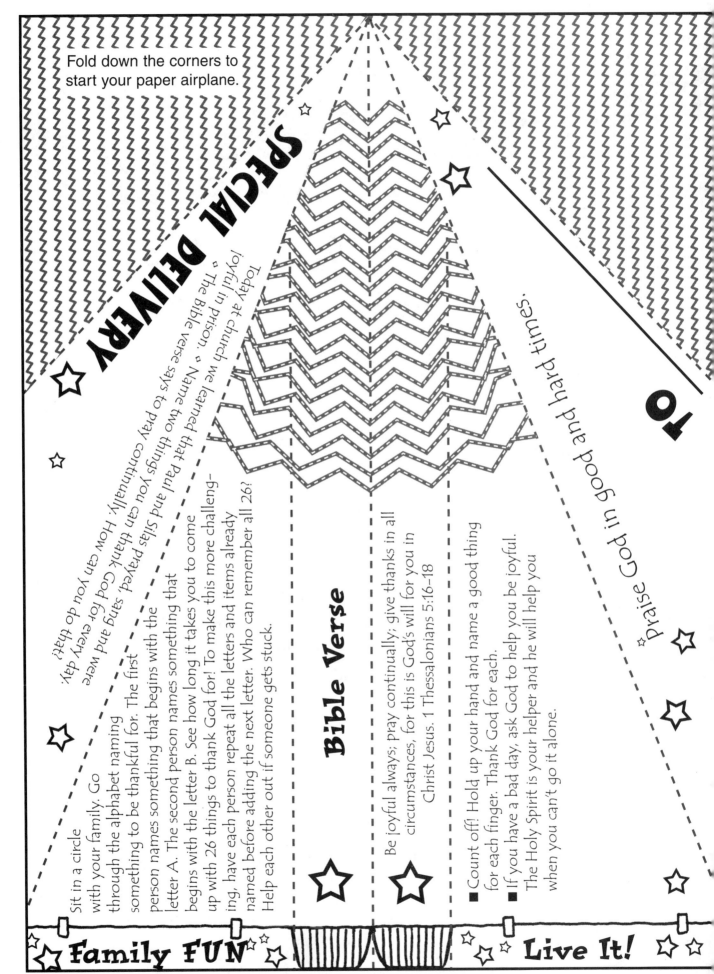

Stake Your Tent on Solid Ground

Option

Get Set
LARGE GROUP ■ Greet kids and do a puppet skit. Schooner discovers the importance of knowing your stuff before teaching others.
❑ large bird puppet ❑ puppeteer

1

Bible 4U! Instant Drama
LARGE GROUP ■ Talking tents share today's Bible story!
❑ 4 actors ❑ copies of pp. 110–111, "Stake Your Tent!" script
❑ 4 numbered balls   Optional: ❑ tent ❑ Bibletime backdrop

2

Shepherd's Spot
SMALL GROUP ■ Use the "Pup Tent" handout to help kids learn that God wants us to learn and obey his Word. Share concerns and pray together. Send home the Special Delivery handout.
❑ Bibles ❑ pencils ❑ scissors ❑ copies of p. 114, "Pup Tent"
❑ copies of p. 116, Special Delivery

Option

Workshop Wonders
SMALL GROUP ■ Kids will make a small, portable book and then jot down ways they can share the joy of God's truth with others.
❑ poster board cut into 6" x 5" pieces ❑ colorful self-adhesive paper cut into 6" x 5" pieces ❑ copy or construction paper ❑ markers or crayons
❑ stapler ❑ pencils ❑ Bibles

Bible Basis
Priscilla and Aquila teach Apollos.
Acts 18:18–21, 24–28

Learn It!
God wants us to understand his Word.

Live It!
Learn and obey God's Word.

Bible Verse
Jesus replied, "If anyone loves me, he will obey my teaching."
John 14:23

Quick Takes

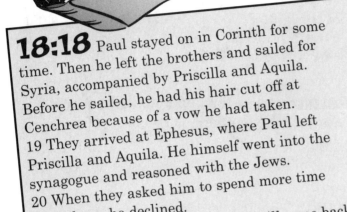

Acts 18:18–21, 24–28

18:18 Paul stayed on in Corinth for some time. Then he left the brothers and sailed for Syria, accompanied by Priscilla and Aquila. Before he sailed, he had his hair cut off at Cenchrea because of a vow he had taken.
19 They arrived at Ephesus, where Paul left Priscilla and Aquila. He himself went into the synagogue and reasoned with the Jews.
20 When they asked him to spend more time with them, he declined.
21 But as he left, he promised, "I will come back if it is God's will." Then he set sail from Ephesus.
24 Meanwhile a Jew named Apollos, a native of Alexandria, came to Ephesus. He was a learned man, with a thorough knowledge of the Scriptures.

25 He had been instructed in the way of the Lord, and he spoke with great fervor and taught about Jesus accurately, though he knew only the baptism of John.
26 He began to speak boldly in the synagogue. When Priscilla and Aquila heard him, they invited him to their home and explained to him the way of God more adequately.
27 When Apollos wanted to go to Achaia, the brothers encouraged him and wrote to the disciples there to welcome him. On arriving, he was a great help to those who by grace had believed.
28 For he vigorously refuted the Jews in public debate, proving from the Scriptures that Jesus was the Christ.

Insights

Paul's years of missionary travel were in strategic places. He usually went to towns that were seaports and centers of trade where diverse culture met and spread out. Corinth and Ephesus were typical Roman capitals, with harbors filled with ships from Egypt, Greece, and Italy. Paul preached and taught in Corinth for about a year and a half. Corinth was a wealthy city; the city imported ivory, wheat, papyrus, and leather. It was also an immoral city, home to the Synagogue of Aphrodite, the Greek goddess of love, with over 1, 000 synagogue prostitutes.

Paul started a church in Corinth and became friends with Aquila and his wife, Priscilla; the three worked together making tents. Priscilla and Aquila followed Paul to the busy port city of Ephesus, home of the goddess Artemis (Diana). Paul traveled on from there to Caesarea, Antioch and other Asia cities while Priscilla and Aquila remained in Ephesus.

After Paul's departure, Apollos arrived in Ephesus and was an impressive speaker. However, Priscilla and Aquila saw immediately that Apollos didn't have the whole story. He argued well from Old Testament passages and knew the teaching of John the Baptist. But he knew nothing of the life of Jesus and the coming of the Holy Spirit. The more experienced believers took Apollos into their home to help him understand God's revelation more fully.

We need to know and understand the Bible well. If we are well grounded, trendy theology and unbiblical thinking will not sway us. When we understand God's Word, we can obey it more wholeheartedly. Like ancient tent-dwellers needed to stake their tents on solid ground, we stake our lives on God's Word. Use today's lesson to encourage children to learn and obey God's Word.

Get Set

Welcome. I'm happy we're together again. It's time to listen, learn, and maybe even laugh a little. Today we hear about three Bible people: a woman named Priscilla, and two men named Aquila and Apollos. Although the names may be new to us, we have a lot to learn from this amazing New Testament team. *Schooner pops up.*

Schooner: Hi, boss.

Leader: Hi, Schooner.

Schooner: Go team!

Leader: Yes, I guess I did use that word.

Schooner: A baseball team! Yea! Can I play centerfield?

Leader: Why centerfield?

Schooner: I'm great at catching fly balls. *(flaps wings)* 'Cause I can fly!

Leader: That's a great idea, Schooner. But I wasn't talking about a baseball team.

Schooner: Oh. A comedy team! That's it. I love to laugh! *Squawk!* Wanna hear a joke?

Leader: No, I wasn't talking about a comedy team.

Schooner: Oh. I get it. It was a singing group.

Leader: What makes you say that?

Schooner: Well, singing groups have strange names.

Leader: You mean Priscilla and Aquila?

Schooner: Those two.

Leader: And Apollos.

Schooner: Right, right, and again, right. What kind of music did they sing?

Leader: They're not a music group, Schooner.

Schooner: No music?

Leader: No music.

Schooner: No comedy?

Leader: No comedy.

Schooner: No baseball?

Leader: No baseball.

Schooner: I'm out of guesses. You'll have to spill the beans, boss.

Leader: Priscilla and Aquila were friends of disciple Paul. They learned from him and traveled with him.

Schooner: Well, it's great they were friends. But how does that make them a team?

Leader: Priscilla and Aquila were a husband and wife team who taught others about the love of Jesus.

Schooner: Teaching is a hard job, boss.

Leader: *(rolls eyes)* And they didn't have a parrot!

Schooner: *(excitedly)* Oooohhh I feel a joke coming on. When you close your eyes, why should it remind you of an empty classroom?

Leader: I don't know Schooner, why should it remind me of an empty classroom?

Schooner: Because you can't see any pupils! Ha, ha, ha! Get it.

Leader: Very funny, Schooner.

Schooner: My friend, Clyde, told me that.

Leader: We can learn a lot from friends. Priscilla and Aquila taught their friends about the Lord Jesus.

Schooner: Name one thing, boss.

Leader: To be a good teacher you need to know your stuff.... To spread the the Word of God you need to know the Word of God.

Schooner: Gotta do that.

Leader: And the truth about Jesus.

Schooner: Gotta do that.

Leader: Priscilla and Aquila learned from Paul, and then they taught Apollos, who became a great teacher to lots and lots of other people.

Schooner: You teach. I learn, boss.

Leader: Be prepared is my motto. When you believe with your heart and mind that Jesus is the way, you want to do a good job telling others. Let's listen to how the story unfolds in Bible 4U!

Printed in Pick Up 'n' Do Lessons on Rise and Shine!: The Early Church

1 Bible 4U!

Welcome to Bible 4U! Theater! Raise your hand if you've ever slept in a tent. Pause for kids to respond.

Today tents are made from nylon or other super light material and made by machine. In Bible times, tent-makers did not have these materials. Tents were made by hand and from animal skins. Many Bible people lived in tents as their homes—unlike today when we use tents mostly for camping trips. In Bible times, being a tentmaker was a good job to have.

Instant Prep

Before class assign three volunteers to play the parts of three talking tents. Have another be the show host. Give each person a copy of "Stake Your Tent" script to review.

The disciple Paul was a tentmaker. While he traveled around as a missionary, he earned money by making tents. Along the way, he met two other tentmakers, Aquila and his wife, Priscilla. But what Paul and his new friends liked doing best was studying God's Word and helping people understand the truth about Jesus. Others wanted to know everything about Jesus and live the way Jesus said to live.

for Overachievers

Have a drama team prepare the story. Use a Bibletime city backdrop with camping gear and set up a tent. Throw tarps over the talking tents. The show host has a microphone and carries the script. Provide bells or buzzers for actors to use before their lines.

These three friends were together in a city called Ephesus. After a while, Paul left town, and a new friend came, named Apollos. Priscilla and Aquila heard him speak for the Lord and loved his enthusiasm. But he only knew half of the story about Jesus. So Priscilla and Aquila invited Apollos to their house to teach him the rest of the story.

In today's drama we hear from three talking tents featured on a TV show called "Stake Your Tent!" That's right, talking tents!

Stake Your Tent!
Based on Acts 18:18-21, 24–28

Three talking tents are on all fours.

Host: Welcome to the show, Stake Your Tent! Our show finds out what's going on in the tent world of today. Here are our contestants. Please tell us your name and where you're staked out.

Teach & Talk: Hi, I'm Teach & Talk. I'm staked out by the synagogue.

Biz: My name is Open for Business. Call me Biz. I hang out in Priscilla and Aquila's tent shop. Someday I'll be sold and get to see the world.

Seen It All: I'm Seen It All! I already see the world. I'm staked by the city gates…so I see everyone who comes in and out of town.

Host: Okay, tents. Here's your first "Tent Trivia" question! Name the most famous recent arrival in Ephesus.

Seen It All: I know, I know! Paul. He came to town to stir things up. I saw him come through the gate myself.

Host: Correct! Question number two: What was Paul's first stop when he came to town?

Teach & Talk: That's right up my alley. He came to the synagogue, of course. That's what he always does.

Host: Correct! Describe Paul's relationship with the people in Ephesus.

Seen It All: I hear all the news. The Christians like him, because he helped them understand the Word of God. They asked him to stay longer, but he had to go.

Host: Correct. Paul promised to come back another time, if it was God's will. Next question: Name a husband and wife team who stayed behind when Paul left Ephesus.

Biz: This one's mine! That would be Priscilla and Aquila, the tentmakers.

Host: Correct! Next question: When they're not in their tent shop, where do Priscilla and Aquila spend their time?

Teach & Talk: I got it! They come to the synagogue to listen to the learned men preach.

Host: Ephesus is a busy city. New people come to town all the time. New question: Name another well-known preaching personality.

Biz: I know this one. That would be Apollos.

Host: Correct! The questions are getting tougher now. I want each of you to tell me one fact about Apollos. Biz, we'll start with you.

Biz: *(thinking nervously)* Let's see…

Host: Hurry. The clock is ticking.

Biz: He came from Egypt!

Host: Correct! Seen It All, give us another fact.

Seen It All: No problem. Apollos had a good education. He liked school.

Host: Correct! Okay, Teach & Talk, it's up to you.

Teach & Talk: He was a bold preacher. He came to the synagogue and talked about God in an amazing way. The crowd really loved him.

Host: Okay, we're ready for the next round. Every question gets harder. Describe Priscilla and Aquila's opinion of Apollos.

Biz: Who would know more about that than I would? I hear them talking every day.

Host: Quick, do you have an answer, Biz?

Biz: Priscilla and Aquila knew Apollos to be a gifted speaker. Apollos knew a lot of Old Testament stories. But he needed to learn more about Jesus. They invited him to their home so they could teach him.

Host: Who can tell me what happened to Apollos after that?

Seen It All: Nothing gets by me. Apollos left Ephesus. He was now eager to speak of the Scriptures that proved Jesus as the Messiah.

Host: Sorry, tents but we're running out of time. It's time for the bonus round. How is being a Christian like being a tent?

Biz: Hmm. Tents give people homes when they have nowhere else to live.

Seen It All: Tents cover people. Christians cover people with love.

Teach & Talk: *(thinking on an answer)* Tents put down stakes so they don't blow away.

Biz: I get what you mean. Tent pegs get pounded into solid ground. Christians have to put their faith in solid ground, the Bible. In this way, they don't follow false teachings.

Seen It All: So, just like a tent stands strong in a storm, Christians put down stakes by learning and obeying God's Word.

Host: All great answers. Now we come to the most important question of our show. What is the one thing you would be willing to stake your tent on today?

All Three: God's Word!

Host: And that's our show for today, folks! Tune in next time, when you'll hear tents share their secrets on waterproofing and interior design. That's next time on everyone's favorite show, *Stake Your Tent!*

Printed in Pick Up 'n' Do Lessons on Rise and Shine!: The Early Church

The people in the early church showed us how important it is to understand and obey God's Word. Paul, Priscilla, Aquila, and Apollos all helped others understand God's Word so they could go on to Christian lives. It is important to know God's Word. We'll need the Bible's truth when the time comes to share it. Let's play some tent trivia with four questions.

Toss the four numbered balls to different parts of the room. Bring kids with the balls to the front one-by-one and ask these questions. Allow kids to get help from the group if they need it. After each correct answer, let kids drop the ball into a bag.

 ■ **Who came to Ephesus with Paul?**

 ■ **What did Priscilla and Aquila do for Apollos?**

 ■ **What was Apollos good at doing?**

 ■ **On your next camping trip remember how learning God's Word is like firmly staking a tent. Share the highlights of today's drama.**

The Bible is the story of how much God loves us. He loved us enough to send his only Son, Jesus, to die on the cross for our sins. When we're sorry for our sins and want to change our ways, we ask Jesus to forgive us. Jesus sends the Holy Spirit into our lives. Everything changes when we become God's children. We become Christians. The Holy Spirit helps us live God's way. Once we know the truth, we live the truth and we share the truth with others.

Read the Bible. If you don't have one, I have one for you. Don't worry if you don't understand everything you read in God's Word. Ask questions. Your parents, Sunday school teachers and pastor can help. Today in your shepherd groups, you'll learn how important it is to obey Jesus.

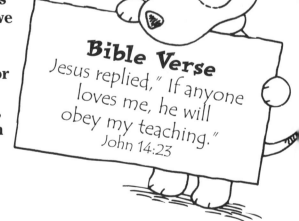

Bible Verse
Jesus replied, "If anyone loves me, he will obey my teaching."
John 14:23

Dismiss kids to their shepherd groups.

2 Shepherd's Spot

Gather your small group and help kids find John 14:23 in their Bibles.

Once we ask Jesus into our lives and begin to understand the Bible, we need to do one more thing. Let's read and see what that is.

Have a volunteer read John 14:23 aloud or read it together: "Jesus replied, 'If anyone loves me, he will obey my teaching."

- **According to this verse, what do we do when we love Jesus?**
- **How do we know what Jesus wants us to do?**
- **What is one thing Jesus taught that you can do as soon as you leave church today? What about at home tonight? Or on the soccer field tomorrow?**

We've been talking about tents today. Paul, Priscilla, and Aquila were tentmakers, and during Bible 4U! three talking tents helped us learn the Bible story. Just as a tent needs to be staked in solid ground or it will blow away, Christians need to know the solid truth of God's Word.

Do you know what people call a very small tent? They call it a pup tent. Let's take a look at a friendly Pup Tent we can make to remind us to learn and obey God's Word, and put strong stakes into solid ground. Pass out the "Pup Tent" handout. Have kids color the tent. Cut out the tent and fold to assemble.

When you take your paper pup tent home today, put it somewhere to remind you to learn and obey God's Word. Have your kids join hands in prayer. Pray for people who don't have God's Word in their own language or who don't own a Bible. Invite kids to share prayer concerns. **Dear Lord, thank you for sending a parent, teacher or friend who shared God's good news with us. Help us to share the good news of Jesus Christ with others. We pray for others who don't have your Word written in their language or who don't own a Bible.** Pause and have kids add names if desired. **Thank you for our Bibles and our church. Please help us learn and obey God's Word this week. In Jesus' name, amen.**

Pup Tent

John 14:23 Jesus replied, "If anyone loves me, he will obey my teaching."

Stake your life on the Word of God.

Instructions:
1. Cut out the pup tent on the solid lines.
2. Fold on the dashed lines.
3. Overlap the bottom tabs and tape them together.

Pup Tent

John 14:23 Jesus replied, "If anyone loves me, he will obey my teaching."

Stake your life on the Word of God!

Instructions:
1. Cut out the pup tent on the solid lines.
2. Fold on the dashed lines.
3. Overlap the bottom tabs and tape them together.

Workshop Wonders

Paul spent his time traveling around teaching others about Jesus. Priscilla and her husband, Aquila, listened to Paul, then took what they learned, and taught Apollos. In the same way, Apollos taught others.

- ■ Name one person who shared the risen Christ with you.
- ■ On busy school and soccer days, what helps you remember to read God's Word?

Let's make a colorful little portable book that will keep God's word on the tip of your tongue!

Get List:

- ❑ poster board cut into 6" x 5" pieces
- ❑ colorful self-adhesive paper cut into 6" x 5" pieces
- ❑ copy or construction paper
- ❑ markers or crayons
- ❑ stapler
- ❑ pencils
- ❑ Bibles

Give each child two pieces of poster board and two pieces of self-adhesive paper cut slightly larger than the poster board. Center the self-adhesive paper over the poster board and snip off each corner. Show kids how to peel the back off of the self-adhesive paper and adhere it to the poster board. Fold the edges over the back side of the poster board. (The cut corners will make perfect mitered corners.) Use this same method to make a book front and a book back.

Finally, give each child two sheets of paper cut in half. Place the paper between the back and front covers and staple along the binding. **Now you have a beautiful book to call your own. Print a title on the cover, such as, "My Book about God." Then on each page inside your book, draw or write something you memorized or know from God's Word. You can also jot down fun ways you can teach others about Jesus—through poetry or songs or dramas or recipes or meaningful Scripture verses. A scrapbook is a very good idea too!**

Take some time to brainstorm with kids and write answers where everyone can see and copy if they wish. You might want to have the kids copy the Bible verse onto a page in the book.

- ■ How will you use your book at home?
- ■ How can you use your book to encourage others to get closer to God?

Ask if anyone would like to share their books with the group. **Take this book home and keep it in a place where it will remind you to learn and obey God's Word.**

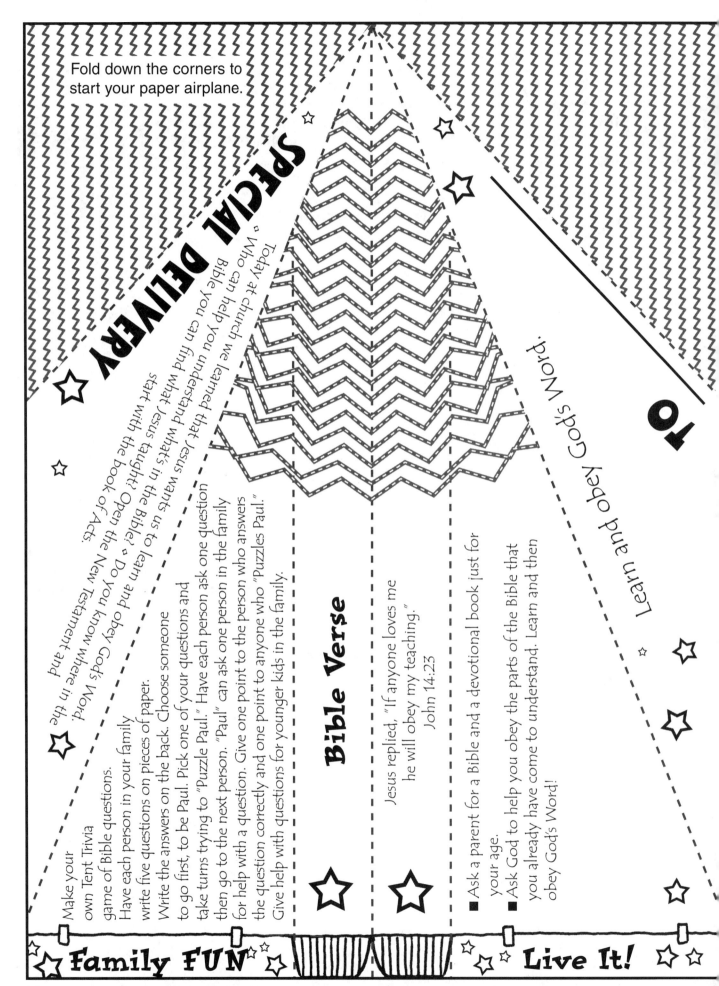

Fold down the corners to start your paper airplane.

SPECIAL DELIVERY

TO

Learn and obey God's Word.

"Who can help you understand what's in the Bible? Open the New Testament and start with the book of Acts. Do you know where in the Bible you can find what Jesus taught?"

Today at church we learned that Jesus wants us to learn and obey God's Word.

Family FUN

Make your own Tent Trivia game of Bible questions. Have each person in your family write five questions on pieces of paper. Write the answers on the back. Choose someone to go first, to be Paul. Pick one of your questions and take turns trying to "Puzzle Paul." Have each person ask one question then go to the next person. "Paul" can ask one person in the family for help with a question. Give one point to the person who answers the question correctly and one point to anyone who "Puzzles Paul." Give help with questions for younger kids in the family.

Bible Verse

Jesus replied, "If anyone loves me he will obey my teaching."
John 14:23

Live It!

- Ask a parent for a Bible and a devotional book just for your age.
- Ask God to help you obey the parts of the Bible that you already have come to understand. Learn and then obey God's Word!

Paul Says Goodbye

Option

Get Set
LARGE GROUP ■ Greet kids and do a puppet skit. Schooner talks about how hard it is to say good-bye to friends.
❑ large bird puppet ❑ puppeteer

1

Bible 4U! Instant Drama
LARGE GROUP ■ Four "Yes, God!" team runners meet up with Coach Paul.
❑ 5 actors ❑ copies of pp. 120–121, "Run a Good Race!" script ❑ 4 numbered balls Optional: ❑ 5 running or sweats outfits with paper race numbers on them, Bibletime or track backdrop, 4 Bibles

2

Shepherd's Spot
SMALL GROUP ■ Make a "Finish the Race" game to take home as a reminder of why we do God's work. Share concerns and pray. Send home the Special Delivery handout,
❑ Bibles ❑ scissors, ❑ tape ❑ copies of p. 124, "Finish the Race!"
❑ copies of p. 126, Special Delivery

Option

Workshop Wonders *
SMALL GROUP ■ End on a sweet note. Use a little elbow grease and make pleasing parfaits to remember the sweet fellowship Paul had with his friends.
❑ cold milk ❑ instant pudding ❑ sandwich cookies ❑ ripe banana slices
❑ large zip top bag ❑ plastic spoons ❑ clear cups ❑ snap lid plastic containers or jars with lids. Optional: ❑ whipped topping and maraschino cherries

*Check with parents for any food allergies children may have.

Bible Basis Paul's farewell speech to the church at Ephesus. Acts 20:17–24, 32, 35–36

Learn It! God wants us to do his work everywhere we go.

Live It! Serve God with your whole life.

Bible Verse I have fought the good fight, I have finished the race, I have kept the faith. 2 Timothy 4:7

Quick Takes

Acts 20:17–24, 32, 35–36

20:17 From Miletus, Paul sent to Ephesus for the elders of the church.

18 When they arrived, he said to them: "You know how I lived the whole time I was with you, from the first day I came into the province of Asia.

19 I served the Lord with great humility and with tears, although I was severely tested by the plots of the Jews.

20 You know that I have not hesitated to preach anything that would be helpful to you but have taught you publicly and from house to house.

21 I have declared to both Jews and Greeks that they must turn to God in repentance and have faith in our Lord Jesus.

22 "And now, compelled by the Spirit, I am going to Jerusalem, not knowing what will happen to me there.

23 "I only know that in every city the Holy Spirit warns me that prison and hardships are facing me.

24 "However, I consider my life worth nothing to me, if only I may finish the race and complete the task the Lord Jesus has given me—the task of testifying to the gospel of God's grace.

32 "Now I commit you to God and to the word of his grace, which can build you up and give you an inheritance among all those who are sanctified.

35 "In everything I did, I showed you that by this kind of hard work we must help the weak, remembering the words the Lord Jesus himself said: 'It is more blessed to give than to receive.'"

36 When he had said this, he knelt down with all of them and prayed.

Insights

Paul was heading back to Jerusalem after his long missionary journeys. He had missed Passover in Jerusalem because of his travels and was anxious to be there for Pentecost 50 days later. Also, he was carrying a generous gift from the Asian churches to the persecuted Christians in Jerusalem. Paul had spent a significant amount of time in Ephesus and was closely connected to the leaders there. He asked them to meet him so he could say good-bye.

Paul knew that danger awaited him in Jerusalem, and so did his friends. Some of them pleaded with him not to make the journey (Acts 21:4, 12). But Paul felt compelled by the Holy Spirit to go to Jerusalem anyway. This gathering was particularly emotional because they did not expect to see each other again. This story is a picture of sweet Christian fellowship between people who had labored together for the gospel.

Paul talked at length to the group, using the analogy of a race. It was a favorite illustration, one that he also used in his written letters to the Corinthians, Galatians and the young pastors, Timothy and Titus. His listeners and readers understood the analogy. Throughout the Roman Empire, men trained vigorously for months to compete in Olympic races. Paul knew that the Christian life required stamina. True discipleship is not for the weak. Despite the dangers ahead of him, Paul followed the urging of the Spirit.

Use today's lesson to encourage kids to serve God wholeheartedly, with their minds, hearts, attitudes, and actions.

Get Set

Hello...and goodbye! How many ways can we say goodbye? Farewell. So long. Bye-bye. Adios. See you later. I have a hard time saying good-bye to my friends, especially the ones I don't see very often. Help us out here, Schooner. *Schooner pops up.*

Schooner: *(comes up singing)* Hello, you say good-bye, I say hello!

Leader: Hello to you, too, Schooner. Today's Bible story, though, is about a goodbye.

Schooner: *(gets serious)* Why do we have to talk about that?

Leader: Goodbye?

Schooner: I don't like saying goodbye.

Leader: *(hugs Schooner)* Sometimes we have to.

Schooner: I still don't like it. It's the end of the fun!

Leader: I understand. Yes, sometimes it is.

Schooner: It's the end of the good times!

Leader: Yes, sometimes it is.

Schooner: It's the end of the world!

Leader: Now, Schooner. That's going a bit too far.

Schooner: *(hangs head)* It's just how I feel.

Leader: Let's think. Is there something that might make goodbyes easier for you?

Schooner: *(thinking)* If I know when I'll see my friend again, I wouldn't feel so bad.

Leader: That's a good point.

Schooner: I know I can send an email or a letter.

Leader: Or call on the phone.

Schooner: Or trade pictures.

Leader: Now you're talking!

Schooner: *(shakes head)* I still don't like to say goodbye.

Leader: Schooner, a goodbye in one place means a hello somewhere else.

Schooner: Hmm.

Leader: Ready to give a listen?

Schooner: Well, okay, let's have it.

Leader: Disciple Paul was on a journey to Jerusalem. But first he had to say goodbye to his friends in Ephesus.

Schooner: Did he like these friends a little or a lot?

Leader: He liked them a lot.

Schooner: Maybe he should have stayed.

Leader: In his heart he wanted to. Paul and his friends at Ephesus had been through many tough times. Too many to count. Still, Paul was sure God wanted him in Jerusalem.

Schooner: Really sure?

Leader: Really sure.

Schooner: Really, really sure?

Leader: Really, really sure.

Schooner: Are you really sure he was really sure?

Leader: You're starting to confuse me, little bird.

Schooner: I just want to be sure.

Leader: In everything Paul did, he showed his friends that hard work helps those who can't help themselves. Just before he left, Paul shared the words of Jesus.

Schooner: Tell me, boss.

Leader: Paul's words were, "It is more blessed to give than to receive."

Schooner: Paul had to say good-bye to his friends because others needed him.

Leader: Very good, Schooner.

Schooner: It didn't keep him from feeling sad though, did it, boss?

Leader: It didn't. But saying goodbye to his friends honored them and showed his love.

Schooner: I've learned a lot from our Bible stories this time around, boss.

Leader: That's a joy to hear, Schooner.

Schooner: *Squawk!* I will remember to pray the next time I say goodbye to a friend. If it helped Paul it will help me too.

Leader: Let's look at how we can run a good race in Bible 4U! up next!

1 Bible 4U!

Welcome to Bible 4U! Theater! Do we have any fast runners here? Pause. **Has anyone ever run in a long race?** Pause. **A marathon is a race 26 miles long. Paul described life as a long race that we run with Jesus. Like a coach for long-distance runners, Paul gives the leaders of the church at Ephesus a pep talk to encourage them to carry on without him. Paul says goodbye because he must leave on a dangerous trip and may not see them again.**

Instant Prep

Before class assign five volunteers their parts. Four are runners and one is Coach Paul. Give each a copy of "Run a Good Race" script to review. Have on hand four Bible for Paul to pass out.

A coach is someone who helps train you do your best. Paul was a wonderful coach for the early Christians. He spent time praying and obeying God. We heard how Paul suffered for the faith, but he never gave up loving Jesus Christ and obeying Father God.

for Overachievers

Have a drama team prepare the story. Dress Paul like a coach, with a whistle around his neck. Dress running team in sweats or workout outfits with "God's Team" and paper race numbers on their front and back. Use either a Bibletime background or running track. Designate a finish line made of ribbon, string or crepe paper. Label it "Finish Line." Have on hand four Bible for Paul to pass out.

The early Christians had a hard life. Paul gave them words of wisdom, advice and comfort to carry on. We, too, need comfort and wise advise. It would be nice to have life all figured out, to not have to put up with bad times and hurt feelings. God leads us when we can't figure things out for ourselves. He leads us through the wisdom of wise and trustworthy people like Paul in today's story. Let's listen to Paul's special words.

Run a Good Race!
Based on Acts 20:17–24, 32, 35–36

Runners jog in and run in place.

Sarah: It's fun to be part of God's Team. That was a good run. I wonder why Coach Paul invited us to meet him here today?

Daniel: I heard he's on his way to Jerusalem. And we have to go back to Ephesus tomorrow.

Jesse: Coach Paul always has great advice. I learned a lot from him in training camp.

Jada: What I remember most? We can serve God wherever we are. Hey, here he comes now.

Coach Paul enters. Joggers stop running in place.

All: Hey, Coach!

Paul: Hey, everybody. It's so good to see you again. I've missed you. Thanks for coming all this way to see me.

Jesse: No problem! You're a best friend. We enjoy being with you.

Paul: Go on and sit. I have a lot to tell you.

They all sit.

Daniel: We're ready to listen.

Paul: You know that I've always tried to help you in any way I can.

Jada: You've been great, Coach.

Paul: I've served the Lord with humility, sometimes with tears. When I'm with you, I teach what I know about believing God, following Jesus, and living the Christian life.

Sarah: That's right, you help us a lot.

Paul: I've gone house to house preaching the risen Jesus.

Jesse: That's how you found me!

Paul: I've talked to both Jews and Gentiles. I've told others to repent and turn to God, and have faith in Jesus.

Daniel: You've trained us well, Coach. Check out my muscles! *(flexes)* I've been working out!

Paul: That's great! You've worked hard and you're ready for the big race.

Jada: All that work is paying off. But what about you?

Paul: I'm headed to Jerusalem.

Daniel: *(hangs head)* We've heard.

Paul: And the Holy Spirit is warning me that prison and more hard times are ahead for me so I may not see you again.

Daniel: Then don't go! Stay here with us.

Paul: The Spirit is telling me to go.

Jada: But, Paul! If you get hurt, what then?

Paul: That's why I wanted to see you today.

Jesse: *(shakes head and pleads)* How can you go to Jerusalem when you know what will happen to you there? I don't understand.

Paul: My life is service to God, to finish the race.

Sarah: *(sighs)* I don't know what to say, Coach.

Paul: Please keep me in your prayers. I want to finish my race and complete the job of telling everyone I meet about the grace of God.

Sarah: But, Coach, if you're leaving, who will help train us?

Paul: God and his Word. They are all you need now.

Daniel: Are you sure we're ready?

Paul: You're in God's care. I'm confident God will care for you with his grace.

Jada: We're going to miss you a lot, Coach.

Paul: I know. But let's keep our eyes on the prize. Heaven is a gift from God to all who run the race well.

Jada: Well, how should we spend our time without you?

Paul: Help the weak.

Sarah: I agree. That's what Jesus would want us to do.

Paul: Jesus himself said, "It is more blessed to give than to receive."

Jesse: It's better to spend our lives giving to others than getting things for ourselves.

Daniel: Do you have any last advice, Coach?

Paul: *(hands each a Bible)* God's training manual. I brought each of you a copy of the Bible to help you grow stronger. But it only works if you read it and heed it.

All: Great! This helps. Thanks, Coach.

Paul: *(hugs Sarah and Jesse)* I couldn't ask for better friends.

Daniel: We feel the same way.

Paul: I'll miss you more than I can say.

Jada: I know you've got to go, Coach. Is there anything we can do for you before you leave?

Paul: Let's pray together. Prayer will help me do the hard things I must do in the city of Jerusalem.

All kneel and pray. Then rise, hug and exit.

Bible 4U!

Paul met with some special friends in this story. He'd spent a lot of time in Ephesus and knew these people well. He had started the church they were all serving in now. Paul and his friends loved each other, and did not want to say goodbye. But Paul knew that saying goodbye was part of running his race for Jesus. See what you can remember about running a good race.

Toss the four numbered balls to different parts of the room. Bring kids with the balls to the front one-by-one and ask these questions. Allow kids to get help from the group if they need it. After each correct answer, let kids drop the ball into a bag.

 ■ What did the Spirit tell Paul would happen in Jerusalem?

 ■ Why did Paul go to Jerusalem anyway?

 ■ What was the last thing Paul did with his friends?

 ■ How does this story help you think about serving God with your words and with your actions?

Paul looked at life as an important race. He trained hard to do his best. Paul didn't choose to serve God only when he felt like it or when he had extra time on his hands. His morning, noons and nights belonged to God.

As followers of Jesus, let's know, grow, and go!

Know Jesus and God's Word.
Grow in faith.
Go tell others that God loves them and gave his Son Jesus for their sins.

Today in your shepherd groups, you'll find that we can serve God in everything we do. Yes, in everything we do!

Dismiss kids to their shepherd groups.

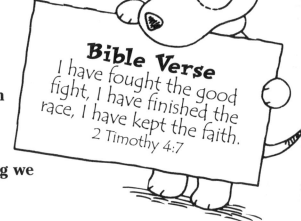

Bible Verse
I have fought the good fight, I have finished the race, I have kept the faith.
2 Timothy 4:7

2 Shepherd's Spot

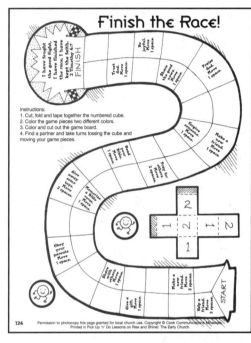

Gather your small group and help kids find 2 Timothy 4:7 in their Bibles.

Before he died, Paul wrote 14 books of the Bible. They were letters he wrote to encourage the people he had been "coaching" in the Christian life. He spent his life telling new Christians how to know, grow, and go. Paul wrote today's Bible verse in a letter to his friend Timothy when he was near the end of his life.

Have a volunteer read 2 Timothy 4:7 aloud.

■ What does it mean "to fight the good fight?" Does it mean using fists? How about to finish the race? How does our loving God help when we are out-of-breath or too tired to go on?

■ Through all the things that Paul suffered for the love of the Lord, how do you think he felt at the end of his life on earth? Was it worth it? Why?

■ Name two things that can help you "finish your race" well.

Paul gave God his very best effort. He didn't hold anything back. He didn't allow danger to scare him off. His faith in Jesus gave him the strength to keep going and serve others.

Let's make a race game to help us remember the good advice we learned from Coach Paul about finishing the race and being faithful in everything we do. Pass out the "Finish the Race!" handout and have kids follow the instructions for assembling and playing with a partner.

Play this game with your family. Talk about ways to serve God together. Let's pray for occasions when we can serve God. Invite kids to share prayer concerns. **Dear Lord, thank you for loving us. We know that we make choices every day, and we can choose to serve you in everything we do.** Pause and have kids pray if desired. **Help us to be a blessing to others this week. Walk with us and grow our love for Jesus, your Son. Help us run a good race. In Jesus' name, amen.**

Finish the Race!

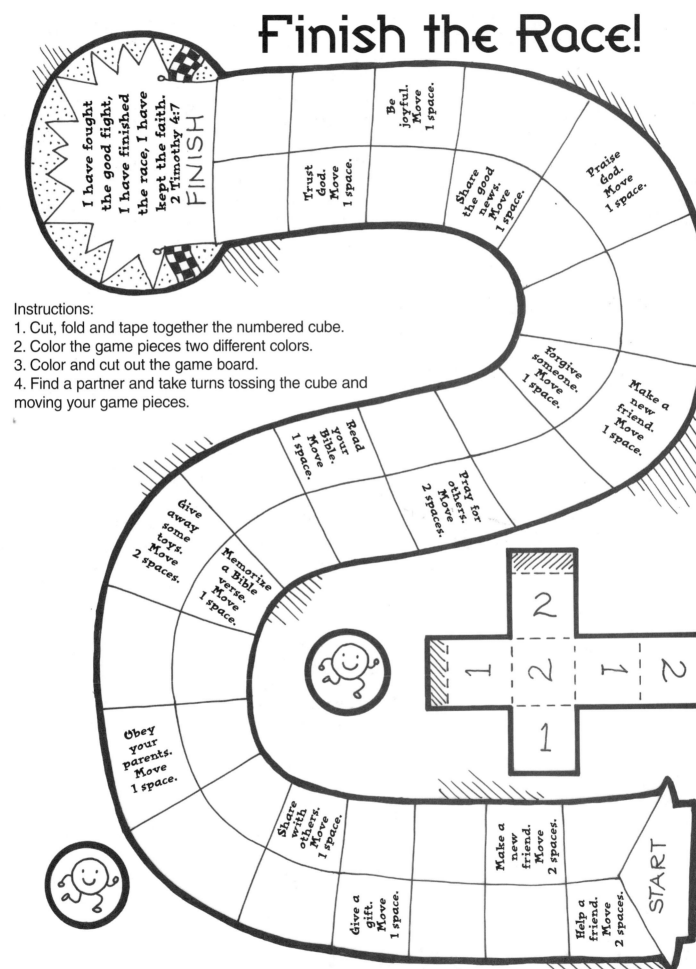

FINISH

I have fought the good fight, I have finished the race, I have kept the faith. 2 Timothy 4:7

Be joyful. Move 1 space.

Trust God. Move 1 space.

Share the good news. Move 1 space.

Praise God. Move 1 space.

Forgive someone. Move 1 space.

Make a new friend. Move 1 space.

Read your Bible. Move 1 space.

Pray for others. Move 2 spaces.

Give away some toys. Move 2 spaces.

Memorize a Bible verse. Move 1 space.

Obey your parents. Move 1 space.

Share with others. Move 1 space.

Give a gift. Move 1 space.

Make a new friend. Move 2 spaces.

Help a friend. Move 2 spaces.

START

Instructions:

1. Cut, fold and tape together the numbered cube.
2. Color the game pieces two different colors.
3. Color and cut out the game board.
4. Find a partner and take turns tossing the cube and moving your game pieces.

Workshop Wonders*

Set out ingredients and containers. Plan on one sealed container, one 1.4-ounce package of instant pudding, and two cups of milk for each four kids.

Get List:
- ❑ cold milk
- ❑ instant pudding
- ❑ sandwich cookies
- ❑ large zip top bag
- ❑ banana slices
- ❑ plastic spoons
- ❑ clear cups
- ❑ snap lid plastic containers or jars with lids

Optional: whipped topping and maraschino cherries

Paul said goodbye to some very good friends. And in Jerusalem he was sure to face imprisonment or death. Paul wanted his dear friends to know that he had no regrets. He worked as hard as he could, with the job God had given him to do. Paul wanted to be an example for others to follow. "See how I did it? Now you do the same."

■ **What hard work have you done for God lately?**

It was hard for Paul to say good-bye to his friends, but it was also a sweet time of fellowship. They prayed together and shared their thoughts with each other. Paul's friends would never forget the experience, and every time they remembered it, they would remember to follow Paul's example to fight the good fight, to finish the race.

Today's sweet parfait treat will take a little work on your part. Pick volunteers to pour the instant pudding and milk, according to directions on the package, into snap lid containers. Have several containers and pudding boxes on hand if you have a large class. Make sure lids are on tight. Gather the group into a circle. Practice saying today's Bible verse aloud. "I have fought the good fight, I have finished the race, I have kept the faith" 2 Timothy 4:7.

Now comes the hard work. When it's your turn, give the container five or six hard shakes. As you do, repeat a part of today's verse. "I have fought the good fight." "I have finished the race," "I have kept the faith." Then pass the container to the next person. The pudding will thicken with each shake.

■ **Have you ever been a runner in a race, or competition, where you really had to push yourself to finish? What helped you keep going?**
■ **Name someone you admire for continuing to work hard for God.** Share an experience of your own. As you do, distribute cups for kids to make their snacks.

Crush chocolate sandwich cookies in a zip top bag. Alternate layers of chocolate pudding, crumbled cookies, and banana slices in cups. Finally, end with a dollop of whipped topping. On goes the sweet ending cherry!

*Check with parents for any food allergies children may have.

Fold down the corners to start your paper airplane.

SPECIAL DELIVERY

TO

☆ Serve God with your whole life.

Today at church, we learned that God wants us to serve him everywhere we go. List some ways that may be new for you! List some ways you can serve God as a family.

Bible Verse

I have fought the good fight, I have finished the race, I have kept the faith. 2 Timothy 4:7

Be a doodle bug! Gather your family and turn everyday doodles into people faces. With a black marker drawer a wide, loose doodle. Trade papers with your family. Take a minute to look at the doodle in front of you. Do you "see" a face? Use a different color marker for eyes, eyeglasses, hair or a mustache. As you work talk about how families can help families in ways that a single individual cannot. Pray together as a family for God's help to run a good race for him.

■ Remember that we can serve God in everything we do.
■ Smile because God loves you. When someone asks why you're smiling, share the good news.

☆ Family FUN ☆   ☆ Live It! ☆

The Word at Work...
Around the World

What would you do if you wanted to share God's love with children on the streets of your city? That's the dilemma David C. Cook faced in 1870s Chicago. His answer was to create literature that would capture children's hearts.

Out of those humble beginnings grew a worldwide ministry that has used literature to proclaim God's love and disciple generation after generation. Cook Communications Ministries is committed to personal discipleship—to helping people of all ages learn God's Word, embrace his salvation, walk in his ways, and minister in his name.

Opportunities—and Crisis

We live in a land of plenty—including plenty of Christian literature! But what about the rest of the world? Jesus commanded, "Go and make disciples of all nations" (Matt. 28:19) and we want to obey this commandment. But how does a publishing organization "go" into all the world?

There are five times as many Christians around the world as there are in North America. Christian workers in many of these countries have no more than a New Testament, or perhaps a single shared copy of the Bible, from which to learn and teach.

We are committed to sharing what God has given us with such Christians.

A vital part of Cook Communications Ministries is our international outreach, Cook Communications Ministries International (CCMI). Your purchase of this book, and of other books and Christian-growth products from Cook, enables CCMI to provide Bibles and Christian literature to people in more than 150 languages in 65 countries.

Cook Communications Ministries is a not-for-profit, self-supporting organization. Revenues from sales of our books, Bible curriculum, and other church and home products not only fund our U.S. ministry, but also fund our CCMI ministry around the world. One hundred percent of donations to CCMI go to our international literature programs.

CCMI reaches out internationally in three ways:

· Our premier International Christian Publishing Institute (ICPI) trains leaders from nationally led publishing houses around the world to develop evangelism and discipleship materials to transform lives in their countries.

· We provide literature for pastors, evangelists, and Christian workers in their national language. We provide study helps for pastors and lay leaders in many parts of the world, such as China, India, Cuba, Iran, and Vietnam.

· We reach people at risk—refugees, AIDS victims, street children, and famine victims—with God's Word. CCMI puts literature that shares the Good News into the hands of people at spiritual risk—people who might die before they hear the name of Jesus and are transformed by his love.

Word Power—God's Power

Faith Kidz, RiverOak, Honor, Life Journey, Victor, NexGen — every time you purchase a book produced by Cook Communications Ministries, you not only meet a vital personal need in your life or in the life of someone you love, but you're also a part of ministering to José in Colombia, Humberto in Chile, Gousa in India, or Lidiane in Brazil. You help make it possible for a pastor in China, a child in Peru, or a mother in West Africa to enjoy a life-changing book. And because you helped, children and adults around the world are learning God's Word and walking in his ways.

Thank you for your partnership in helping to disciple the world. May God bless you with the power of his Word in your life.

For more information about our international ministries, visit www.ccmi.org.